Illustrious

2019 Poetry Collection

Published by
The America Library of Poetry
P.O. Box 978
Houlton, ME 04730
Website: www.libraryofpoetry.com
Email: generalinquiries@libraryofpoetry.com

Printed in the United States of America.

THE AMERICA
LIBRARY OF POETRY

ISBN: 978-0-9966841-5-6

Contents

Poetry by Division

Illustrious

Foreword

There are two kinds of writers in the world.
There are those who write from experience,
and those who write from imagination.
The experienced, offer words that are a reflection of their lives.
The triumphs they have enjoyed, the heartaches they have endured;
all the things that have made them who they are,
they graciously share with us, as a way of sharing themselves,
and in doing so, give us, as readers, someone to whom we may relate,
as well as fresh new perspectives
on what may be our common circumstances in life.
From the imaginative,
come all the wonderful things we have yet to experience;
from sights unseen, to sounds unheard.
They encourage us to explore the limitless possibilities
of our dreams and fantasies,
and aid us in escaping, if only temporarily,
the confines of reality and the rules of society.
To each, we owe a debt of gratitude;
and rightfully so, as each provides a service of equal importance.
Yet, without the other, neither can be truly beneficial.
For instance, one may succeed in accumulating a lifetime of experience,
only to consider it all to have been predictable and unfulfilling,
if denied the chance to chase a dream or two along the way.
Just as those whose imaginations run away with them never to return,
may find that without solid footing in the real world,
life in fantasyland is empty.
As you now embark, dear reader,
upon your journey through these words to remember,
you are about to be treated to both heartfelt tales of experience,
and captivating adventures of imagination.
It is our pleasure to present them for your enjoyment.
To our many authors,
who so proudly represent the two kinds of writers in the world,
we dedicate this book, and offer our sincere thanks;
for now, possibly more than ever,
the world needs you both.

Paul Wilson Charles
Editor

Editor's Choice Award

The Editor's Choice Award is presented
to an author who demonstrates not only
the solid fundamentals of creative writing,
but also the ability to elicit an emotional response
or provide a thought provoking body of work
in a manner which is both clear and concise.

You will find "Connections"
by John Murrell on page 89 of Illustrious

2019
Spirit of Education
For Outstanding Participation

Ernest Becker
Middle School

Las Vegas,
Nevada

Presented to participating students and faculty
in recognition of your commitment
to literary excellence.

Division I

Grades
3-5

My Dog
by Emily Crecelius

My dog is feisty and scary.
She likes to give kisses, but likes to look for food.
She is cute and has a little dot on her head.
She likes to protect my mom, but I love her so.

Spring
by Maddelyn Deeren

The sun is out
The birds are about
Hear me shout
The sun will help plants grow
If you have a bow
Put it in the soil
And watch it grow
You might want to play
Maybe all day
Go outside and play today

The Imagination
by Madelyn Paul

Come with me
And you will see,
A city of buildings,
Where a new world begins,
And here things will be different
Than what you thought to be
Sometimes loud,
Sometimes quiet,
Dream of what
You want it to be

School
by Andrea Chuang

I go to school and I think it's cool.
I like to follow all the rules.
Even if they're not cool.
At school I am always happy.
And it's never sappy.
My teachers are the best.
They work so hard they never take a rest.
When they are tired they never sigh.
But I know someday I will have to say goodbye.
Or not

Coondog
by Miriam Bantrager

Bark, brown, play, dig, scratch
Pretty, run, white, sniff, scared, jump
Black, growl, bite, listen
Collar, water, food, paw, tail
Claws, eye, nose, teeth, name, girl, breath

Sunlight
by Baylee Randall-Hurt

Something catches my eye.
A dog getting her mouth wired shut.
Off to the pound like a prison.
Rescue the dog.
Take her to the vet.
Remove the wires.
Take her home, feed her, water her.
Now called Sunlight.
She is free.

Drama
by Sylvie Larch

Drama this and drama that.
She said this and he said that.
People, people can't you see?
Drama makes me want to flee!
Friendships broken, people mad.
Oh, this is flat out bad!
Plug your ears and close your eyes,
People start to yell big lies.
She is dumb and he is mean.
Drama makes me want to scream!

Foxy
by Kaya Philson

Foxy here, Foxy there,
"Foxy, you're everywhere!"
Foxy left, Foxy right,
"Foxy is out of sight!"
Look here, look there,
"Foxy is nowhere!"
"Oh please, oh please.
Foxy come back to me!"
"Foxy, Foxy in the tree.
Foxy, Foxy why are you hiding from me?"

Skills
by Charis Strong

Coming back to what I know,
I would really like to show,
What my skills can do at most.
I really do not mean to boast,
Moving through the wondrous show,
Going where I want to go ...
Knowing when to show my best.
Knowing when to take a rest.
Finding how far my skills go,
feeling just the soft swift whoa,
The wind whistles upon me.
As I see all my friend's glee,
I bend down onto my knee.
Coming along the fence with them,
My friend, they're the one.
Stars are hiding as a gem,
In the midst of morning sun.
We wonder where the stars go hide,
The gap should never be so wide ...

Waiting For the Sunrise
by Emma Heinzelmann

It has been a million years
Waiting for the sunrise
The wonderful pinks and oranges
Before I see it in the sky
It has been a century
Since I have seen stars
A majestic shining light in the black sky
A clear night sky that heals scars
Another million years
Since I have seen the sea
The salty breeze and lapping waves
It seems to be waiting for me
A few centuries
Since I have seen the hills
The tall grassy hills
With winds that sound like violins
I am also waiting for
A friend that understands
A teacher that gives
And a family that takes you with open hands
After what seems like a decade,
A millennia several centuries
Anything can happen,
And bring back memories

Toes
by Natalee Strathman

Some people ask, "What's the best part of you?" I say back, "My toes!"
Then, they say, "Why is that the best part of you?"
Here is how I explain it.
When I wake up in the morning and get out of bed
the first thing I hear is my toes hitting the floor -tik-tap-tak-tip.
My toes are amazing
Then because my toes are as smart as a scientist
they know when I am late for school and they have to hurry and scurry.
My toes are amazing
When I am not late they may be more slow
they're short, small, and super.
My toes are AMAZING
When I go to dance they're graceful, they leap
they're a piece of talented, tangoing, tough, toes,
when I dance they make a -thap-click-clack-tad
They can be filthy or fancy.
My toes are amazing
At the end of the day when I am lying in bed my toes think,
"I am a Giant. I help everyone balance their own journeys."
When I fall asleep they could wiggle
They are small and short but my toes are really amazing

Friendship
by Dakota Shipley

Friendship can be worth more than wealth and can be more than it's felt
Love is stronger than any other and can break the strongest curse,
as long as it isn't worse
It is easy to walk between the lines, but what adventure will you find
Friendship shows caring and loving and shows others where they're going
Sometimes life isn't clear, but with friends, it may appear
If it all starts with a spark, it can all end with the start.
All it takes is a little courage to say, and then it will stay
Journeys will start to curve into other great whirls
Help will be in your hearts with the others at the start.
Be grateful for who you have and do not try to go past
Years can be forgetful, years can be fearful but you shall make it with the spark
The spark is love, courage, and magic
made from the others who you may be tragic
We are still going through the light with others by our side
Love goes on and on and never waits to be gone
Most is not simple nor is it clear, but it can all be here
Open your eyes and let people come, to give love that will never be gone
Never go into dark thoughts, keep going to where courage goes
Friendship is here and will forever last even at the last
Always remember those who showed care and sparks too
Friendship will never lurch

The Brightest Sun
by Christine O. Njoku

The sun shines so bright in the blue sky
Shines brighter than the moon
Shines brighter than the stars
The brightest sun has ever seen is up looking at me.

Tick Tock
by Tristan Calvez

Once I fall asleep
My clock sits waiting to beep.
While I toss and turn my clock sits firm,
Waiting for 7:00 A.M.
At five o'clock I hear a knock,
And have fallen out of bed.
I climb back in and fall asleep,
Waiting for that beep.
One hour later at six o'clock,
Still tossing and turning.
Sleeping in bed,
Waiting and waiting.
Another hour has passed and now it's time,
Soon to be at school learning.
I hear the clock beep and leap out of bed
No longer asleep and get ready for the ...
Morning!

Hamilton's Last Stand
by Victoria Nelms

I sailed across the Hudson this morning to be here at the crack of dawn.
The sun shone through the branches highlighting the river,
a soft breeze rustled the leaves.
Burr, my first friend, yet my first enemy
stood in front of me with a gun in his outstretched hand.
I stood in front of him too with a gun in my outstretched hand as well.
That one pamphlet I published brought us here.
I said and wrote some remarks about his character.
He wrote me a letter demanding an apology about everything I said.
I refused,
Which caused the arrangements for this duel.
We stared each other in the eyes
when the man beside us started counting to ten,
"One, two, three, four, five, six, seven, eight, nine," I raise my gun at the sky,
"TEN!"
"BOOM!" That bullet was my legacy,
And my last stand as Alexander Hamilton.

Sad Cat Pat
by Makiah Couse

The fat cat Pat had a hat.
The cat had two hats.
The fat cat Pat was sad his friend Matt
had to move to South Platt.

The Wind
by Sara Goheen

The wind blows through the night
and the stars shine so bright.
In the night, there's not a peep
because everyone is sound asleep.
Still is silent in the night
but something is still so bright.
Out and about at night
the grass is singing somewhere high,
about to reach the gleaming sky.
Something blew that night.
Oh what a wonderful sight.
The wind blew so hard
that I could feel it through me.
I didn't know what to do, I had one choice
and that was to go through.
How did I go through you say.
Well the singing grass led the way.

A Trip To Waterloo
by Jing-Yi Hu

Let's go to Waterloo, we could go see Granny Sue.
Said my friend Lou, from Timbuktu.
Just this once I will ask, I will do any task.
I told you no, I've got a show,
Go feed a crow, or beg Uncle Joe.
There's no way I'm going to Waterloo, to see Granny Sue just for you.
I went to the store, I did much more.
I did the dishes, I blessed my wishes.
Now we must leave for Waterloo,
Come on, my friend Drew.
For I told you no, but wait.
If you do my chores.
And much, much more.
Do my homework, do my schoolwork.
Then we might have your trip to Waterloo.
I will do anything for you,
Just for a trip to Waterloo.

The Pencil
by Dylan Moen

If you stick a pencil up your nose you will hit the gold
If you stick it up more you will hit the metal
If you stick it up more you will hit the concrete
If you stick it up more you will hit the blood
If you stick it up more you will have no more pencil left. Why! Why!
My pencil is yellow, it's special, it tastes like a pencil.

Basketball
by Samuel Martin

Basketball is a sport for you and me
It's full of concentration as you may plainly see
They call it Basketball
When people play outside it's so mesmerizing
This sport is very uprising
When they do a crossover it's surprising
They call it Basketball
This is the winter sport
While kids and adults are busy building forts
With the toddlers dressed up totes adorbs
I'm playin' Basketball
When the game has ended and it's time to go
I shoot one last shot, a free throw
It goes through the net as slick as can be
Then others try to make it like me
I love Basketball

Seasons of the Year
by Willa VanLoon

Snow is falling,
Winter's calling.
So let us bundle up to play,
In this cold and snowy gray.
Birds are chirping,
Spring is lurking.
So let us say hooray,
and smell the flowers of May.
Waves are beating,
Summer's heating.
With warm and sunny rays,
we swim and splash in play.
Leaves are falling,
Autumn's calling.
We ride on a wagon of hay,
throughout a colorful day.

The Five Senses
by Camdyn Patzer

I feel, the salty air sting my skin like 1000 fire ants.
I smell, the salty air rising from the ocean.
I taste the burning salt water on my lips.
I hear the ocean crashing against the sand and the seagulls cawing above me.
I see the never-ending ocean in front of me.
This is paradise.

School
by Charley Coffin

I don't want to go to school,
I'd rather go to the pool.
I could play hooky,
at that I'm not a rookie.
You think I could pull it off?
Maybe add a fake cough?
I might miss a scary test,
boy, that would be the best!
But, I won't see my friends,
and our friendship might end.
Oh no!
Should I go?
I miss school.
It's really cool!
I don't know.
I think I will go.

I Don't Get Paid Enough For Chores
by Zeynab Tashtanova

I don't get paid enough for chores
I scrub and scrub the kitchen floors
I ask and ask for more and more
But I never get paid enough
I don't get paid enough for chores
I mow the lawn, up until dawn
I rake the leaves that fell from the trees
I make our meals I'm head over heels
I feed the birds not saying a word
I work and work, while they laugh and smirk
I don't get a dime for my time,
I don't get paid enough for chores
I ask for more money for my chores
But they look at me like I'm a corpse
We are always at war when it comes to mopping the floors,
Because I never get paid enough for chores.

My Bonkers Brother
by Nysha Ghelani

My brother's annoyance
Is filled with avoidance
My brother is a sock
Filled with chalk
My brother smells like rotten eggs in a leg
My brother is a talking brat with a mat on his hat

My Dog
by Hudson Shore

Trooper trooper
Super trooper
You are my dog,
Even though you are dead.
You stay in my head,
You are under my bed
You sleep with me,
I miss you,
I bet you miss me.
And you are not dead to me,
You are still right beside me when I am sad.
And you comfort me,
When I am sad.
Someday, just someday,
I will join you,
And the Holy Lord.

My Best Friend
by Ambria Hubbard

If I was a flower,
I'd want to grow high,
Everyone would look at my beauty,
All in awe.
But when the clouds cover the sunlight,
And the harsh storm makes my petals fall,
I droop down,
And no one sees my beauty anymore.
Except for one,
Who is always so tender and loving,
Sees my inner beauty,
And nurtures me back alive.
Restoring my beauty,
I no longer praise for others to look,
Because I know,
Only one truly cares

The Prophecy
by Henry Nanzer

When even time grows old, it will still be there.
When the darkness comes, it will still be there.
When reality collapses, it will still be there.
Watching us,
listening to us,
Waiting for us.

Wonderland
by Emma Ulmer

I know a place to go,
that no one else will ever know.
You and me,
feeling free.
Tick tock
goes the clock,
showing the wrong time,
in a frame as green as a lime.
Fish fly
in the sky,
and birds swim in the ocean,
in a fast motion.
People walk upside down,
when they are in town.
I know a place to go,
that no one else will ever know.

$100 Or $1,000,000
by Benny Dawson

I got twenty offers for my cars,
And most of them offered the same amount.
"One hundred dollars," they said.
And they all left- without the keys.
The reason I did this was true,
As it was my oldest car.
The first Model T Ford, made on the assembly line,
And wanted it in a museum.
Then, what luck did I have,
A man from the Smithsonian museum came.
"One million dollars, plus repairs," he said.
And he left- with the keys.
One million dollars, I went to check,
Was enough to buy a Ferrari.
Bought one, and went too fast,
Nearly went off the overpass.

The Wrench
by Shelby Theut

I speak Dutch
I am a wrench
I come from a ditch
I am very rich
Are you a snitch?
Do you like to pitch?
I'm going to hitch a ride
even though I have an itch.

Why Would You Give a Child Fifteen Pickles
by Skyler Quinn

Pickle one because it's fun,
Pickle two, you know it dude,
Pickle three made me pee,
Pickle four, are there more,
Pickle five tasted alive,
Pickle six was good as Twix,
Pickle seven, I'm in Heaven,
Pickle eight tasted great,
Pickle nine blew my mind,
Pickle ten, let's do it again,
Pickle eleven was named Kevin,
Pickle twelve, I'll keep it to myself,
Pickle thirteen was very clean,
Pickle fourteen was in a pickle scene,
Fifteen pickles, now I am done, this is all the pickle fun!

Swimming Free
by Allison Walburn

When I go to swim practice after school, I feel a fresh start staring at me.
It's a new day just for me.
When I jump in the water, I feel absolutely free.
The water feels nice, it's just right for me.
We start with a 500 skip and now we're all swimming free.
Steady but fast, I feel like a fish swimming steadily,
but yet like a wolf leading the pack.
Swimming is my most favorite sport, can't you see.
Every lap, every set we do our best even if we burn with pain.
I swim and swim until practice ends.
I feel great at the end when all the pain ends.
While you are changing you hear the water thrashing
and you can smell the chlorine, it's my most favorite smell.
That's the end of swim practice for me.
I hope you, as well, feel free and dive right in with me.

Choose Kind
by Jadin Ross

Choose kind now and forever
Choose kind through thick and thin
Choose kind whatever you do
Choose kind from within
Choose kind everywhere you go
Choose kind in all the hallways
Choose kind and show it everywhere
Choose kind now and always

Nature Is Big
by Riley Ingersoll

Nature is red
Nature is blue
Nature is to see and to do
Nature to me is
Beautiful to see
Nature has become
A part of me
Nature is the wind
Blowing in the leaves
Nature is the rain
Growing in the trees
Nature is the sun
Shining so bright
Nature is a mighty
And powerful sight

The Amazing Game
by Domenic Fredrickson

Thwack!
I heard the crack of the bat.
I heard the crowd roar.
Home run!
The smell of hotdogs and popcorn fill the air.
This can only mean one thing.
Baseball season is here.
The grass is fresh and green.
The sun is yellow and bright.
The dirt flies in our face.
It won't stop us from playing tonight.
Being with my friends.
Playing the greatest game.
Winning or losing.
We love it just the same.

Voting Day
by Sophie Reading

Today is voting day
People stand outside for their turn to vote
Trying to get in and out
Keeping their votes to themselves
While they wait in line for hours
Some parents bring their children only to hear them moan and groan
Then whenever it's their turn to vote, they say hooray
They make their vote and leave without a trace
When they get home they feel relieved that voting day is over

The Girl
by Netra Arora

There's a girl with red nails
Just like rubies shining in the sun
She's sitting next to me
Oh they're so beautiful compared to mine.
Mine are regular and boring purple.
She has beautiful, long hair just like a princess
Compared to mine.
Mine is so short and regular
She has beautiful gray eyes
Compared to mine.
Mine are so boring and dark
Who is that girl, she is so pretty
Oh is that you
I didn't recognize you, let's go play!

Spring Is Here
by Adam Ghanem

Glistening waterfalls blazing golden hot sun
Refreshing air cruising along my face
Emerald plants and hot pink flowers
Soaring birds in the light blue sky
Glamorous aqua water, bronze rocks
People sunbathing in the boiling sun
Such pleasant views of the leafy trees
Will it ever be cold?
What else would I do on this fine spring day?
Children playing everywhere
April showers bring May flowers
Women drinking different drinks
I can see the marvelous clouds in the sky
I can hear voices in the wind talking to me
I never want spring to leave and I hope it never does

Golfing
by Luke Kilcrease

Waiting, walking
pow pop
there goes the ball
Straight through the wind
and onto the green
pop
went into the hole
Laughing, playing, jumping, running
there I go
back to home.

Wishes
by Iris Nieland

When you make a wish,
Does it go up to join the stars?
Or does it fret, like an old guitar?
What happens to wishes gone awry?
Do they mold like cherry pie?
Or do they yell a battle cry?
Flutter down and slowly die?
Maybe you trim 'em down.
Like a dreamy bonsai?
What happens to wishes that are just right,
Perfect, amazing, Turkish delights?
Those come back to you in the night,
And whisper softly,
Goodnight.

All About Bullying
by Trinity Barnett

A bully is a boy or girl who makes you feel bad,
and says things or does things that make you feel sad.
A bully may laugh when you make a mistake or call you mean names,
push you, shove you or shake you.
What do you do if you are bullied today?
You must try to stay calm and just walk away.
Go tell a grownup, they will know what to do.
Teachers and parents are there to help you.
What if you see a bully picking on a friend?
How do you make the meanness come to an end?
Tell the bully to stop! Take your friend by the hand;
go find a grown-up, they will understand.
School is a safe place to learn, grow and play.
If you speak up and stand up, bullies can't ruin the day.

Kitties
by Elizabeth Deuby

For my birthday I would like a kitty,
But no one seems to just take pity,
For years I've kept it in my throat,
But now that I must wear a coat,
It blurted out with eagerness,
I'm not as perfect as a princess,
I know that rhymes are not my thing,
But I'll love the cat as it loves string,
So I guess what I am trying to ask,
Is something hidden that needs no mask.

Forgiveness
by Alivia McDaniel

When people say hurtful things
You should forgive them.
When friends leave you out
You should forgive them anyway.
When someone hurts you
You should forgive them in the end.
If someone bullies you
You should still forgive them.
If someone hurts your feelings
You should still forgive them.
When someone was really mad at me
I forgave them after.
When someone yells at me
I still would forgive them.

Explanations
by Chloe Hemmerich

If love is love, then what is hate?
The dark mist beyond the world?
If hate is hate then what is love?
The warmth inside one's heart?
If darkness is darkness, then what is fate?
What one thinks is their destiny?
If fate is fate, then what is darkness?
The blackness behind a person's eyes?
If evil is evil, then what is a king of lies?
The evil upon thyself?
If a heart is a heart, then what is a rose?
Beauty upon which the eye looks?
If a rose is a rose, then what is a heart?
Where one's thoughts are held close?

My Best Friend
by Alysia G. Due

She always inspires me to do my best,
I need to walk up straight and puff up my chest
She comes in all different forms,
Plays in college dorms,
Sometimes is very lyrical,
Or sometimes is spiritual.
She gets me through hard times,
And just to let you know, she's all mine.
She always makes me laugh,
I still listen to her in the bath.
She allows me to cry,
When we had to say good-bye.
And her name is Music

Life
by Felicity Harris

Life is nice and fills us with flight
Life's a ride that goes through the night
Life is a gift that lifts our spirits
Life is nature and that is better than death
Life is enjoyable which is doable
Life is misleading but I'm still believing
Life is a knife that stabs you in the back
Life holds you tight in its hands of lies
Life can be dark but bright with light
Life is a pain which is a shame
Life has illness and that is madness
Life is a tizzy which leaves me dizzy

Monkeys In Pajamas
by Jake Benner

One day I get on a flying tiger with a monkey in pajamas.
His name is Barnibee.
We get on the tiger and go up like a rocket going to space.
"THUD!" Barnibee! I got off the tiger like a hot potato.
But it was too late, he was gone.
Then he moved a little.
Barnibee? "SPLAT!" what was that for!?
He gave me one of those what do you mean looks.
His splatter spit felt gross on my face which was feeling
Green.
I could feel the brisk fall air tap my face.
Then he stood up, brushed off the dirt and went inside his house
So I went back to my tree.

Nature
by Max Holstein

Trees as green as can be
As tall as the eye can see
As beautiful as the wailing green

A Monster
by Baileigh Lopez

Hey! There's a monster behind my lamp
And it looks like a slimy monster.
It has googly eyes and big, giant feet.
And red hair and a big mouth and a big nose.

Sneaky Pug
by Abby Ringuette

Sneaky pug,
A good bandit,
Stealing food day and night,
My cute puggy.

What I See
by Liam Turner

I shall look at the petals on a flower
I shall look at the nice green grass
I shall look at the nice blue water
I shall look at everything till everything looks at me

Tom Brady
by Rowan Smith

He is so shady, Tom Brady
Does he even have a lady?
Even though he plays football
He could be a big goofball
He has a big diet
And he is always on a riot
He just won the Superbowl
And he is on a role
All he does is win
But he eats from a cookie tin
To finish he has pride
Even though last year he lied

Friends
by Colbie Chewning

Friends
Friendly, understanding
Loving, hugging, cheering
Always your friend!

The Man In the Hat
by Andy Kyle

There once was a man named Nat.
He slept upside down in bed.
He wound up on someone's head.
The person's name was Pat.

Snow
by Brennon Rommeck

When I see snow I think no
When I see rain I know pain
When I see mud I think dud
When I see heat I think I know meat
When I see a cloud I feel proud

The Cat
by Estrella Rodriguez-Espino

I have a pet cat, she loves to sit and sleep, for she is Greek.
My cat Mat is fat, she can be flat,
You never can trust Mat for she is 'Wack'
She loves to eat snails in her pails,
That shall be my cat Mat.

Parents' Life
by Marisa Jimenez

Parents are always busy
that's why they are always drowsy.
Parents pay money
and sometimes are so funny.
My parents are the best
including the rest.
Parents help with children's homework,
and go to work.
Parents are lovable
and sometimes trouble.
Parents are always busy
because they have responsibilities!

Friendship
by Harper Arrant

You make me smile so big,
You make me laugh so hard,
You are so crazy when I'm there and,
not,
You are the cherry to my ice cream and,
The water to my meal,
I don't know what my life would be like without you
always near.

Nature Beauty
by Katie Finney

Streams are flowing.
The breezes are blowing.
Leaves are whistling in my ears.
Bushes bristling against each other.
Critters are crawling.
Leaves are no longer falling.
Spring days are blooming away.
It gets prettier day by day.

Pill Power
by Clayton Grubbs

Schil went to Bill
To get some pills
They were pretty sour
so it took an hour
At the end she was
already feeling better
She said, "Boy, those were sour
but they sure had power!"

Summer
by Ana Robles

Swimming, sunny days and popsicles
Let the waves strike against you
Let the sand get in between your toes
Enjoy the breezy air, and enjoy the weather
Never forget the love of summer
Don't worry about doing homework,
Lean back and enjoy yourself
Go to summer camp, make new friends!
Have a great summer!

Bullfrogs
by Giovanni Munoz

Slimy, green, big, stretch
Jump, far, bumpy, rivers, pond
Mud, water, swamp, brown
Camouflage, stretchy, bugs, flies
Logs, tadpoles, cattails, wet, legs

My Cat
by Shyann Monreal

She is like a superhero.
She can fly without wings.
I love her more than anything in the world.
I wonder what she does at night.
She is fuzzy and soft.
Meow, meow.

Bruce
by Liberty Michael

The dogs in the summer.
The dogs in the fall.
They may not be perfect,
But I love them all.
Winter and spring, they are still around,
But not Bruce ... the only mutt I thought I would ever need as a friend.

The Game of War
by Krue Humphrey

War goes boom
Zooming in the truck
Leveling up
To get more luck.
Up all night
I'm ready to fight
The Nazis are coming
My soldier is running.
We're in a fright
To survive the night
Blurry eyes and a sore thumb
The game is over, I have won.

Say Something
by Faith Crandell

Say something
Anything will do
Speak up,
Some people are counting on you.
If you keep it all to yourself,
No one will know what you're capable of,
Say something,
You are capable of so much more,
Than to keep it all to yourself.
So say something,
It matters more than you think.

First Day of School
by Diya Jonnalagadda

What do we do on our first day of school,
Do we go swimming in a swimming pool?
Or maybe play games all day,
Or go outside to play
Do we paint the nails on our fingers,
Or create a smell that really lingers?
Do we scream so loud,
That it can be heard above a cloud?
I went to school on my first day,
And I was surprised to say that we don't do much play.
I will say school is not so bad,
I am actually pretty glad.

Rodeo
by April Forester

April Marie Forester
Helpful, brave and passionate
Daughter of Randy and Linsey Forester
Who loves family, animals and rodeo
Who feels awesome about rodeo
Who needs Jesus, food and love
Who gives love, fun and family
Who fears snakes, storms and failing
Who would like to see my mom's side of the family
Who dreams to be a rich and famous barrel racer
A student of Eugene Ware
April May

Teddy
by Vaughn Fields

Matted mop of fuzz
On guard, chasing cars
Who lies atop the front door rug
Bringing us a hug
Outside he's running
Barking at dogs
He comes in all muddy
Munching on leaves
Growling when doors shut
He's red as Mars
It's our Teddy dog

My Teacher Is A Dragon
by Zara Kanjwal

My teacher is a dragon
She eats rabbit stew
She has a long tail about 6'2"
She breathes out fire
She inhales smoke
She coughs out clouds
She drinks Diet Coke
She never smiles
She never laughs
She always forgets to take her baths
My teacher is a dragon

Hawaii
by Karin Kobayashi

Hawaii has a lot of pine trees.
The ocean has a good breeze.
I like how Hawaii has a lot of flowers.
There are also a lot of towers.
When I go to the beach, I like to make castles with sand.
I have a lot of things planned.
Hawaii has a lot of mountains.
I always see a lot of water fountains.
I get the lei from the hotel I stay.
I'm planning to build a lot of sandcastles this year.
Or, I might start learning swimming without fear.

I Am a Peacock
by Marley Raymond

I make loud and weird noises.
I have clawed feet.
I have wings and feathers.
I live in a zoo.
My actual home is in Africa.
I am pretty and colorful.
I am a ... peacock.

Cats and Dogs
by Ellison Grinnell

Cats
small, fearful
meowing, clawing, purring
litter box, fur, treats, kennel
barking, biting, licking
big, brave
Dogs

Penguin, Penguin, My Penguin
by Maria Kim

Penguin, penguin, my penguin
I like you a lot when you sleep with me
Penguin, penguin, my penguin
I love to play with you
Penguin, penguin, my penguin
I want you to be with me
Always.

In My Eyes
by Madeline Crandell

In my eyes, we never lose hope.
Even when all is lost.
In my eyes, we always can.
Even when it seems impossible.
In my eyes, we are always brave.
Even at the darkest times.
In my eyes, we are all heroes
Even if we don't have a cape.
In my eyes, we can all do great things.
We just have to do them.

Winter Is Here
by Andrej Rumenovski

cold, frosty winter
I love to play in the snow
and could get frostbite

The Heart
by Avery Buessing

My heart is as big as an elephant but as strong as a lion.
My heart is as big as the human head!
It beats, it thumps, it pumps. It goes puh-dumps.
It is as healthy as us humans. My heart is a healthy heart.
My heart is gigantic, healthy, real, strong, and fierce.
It beats, it goes boom, it pounds. My heart is a fighting heart.
It is strong. It is brave. It is as kind as us humans. It is fierce.

Luna
by Camden Widenmier

When you say fat,
you don't think cat
When you say lumpy,
you don't think frumpy
When you combine those,
it can keep you on your toes
But I love it anyway,
I don't care what you say
Luna, you bring a smile to my face,
Luna, you are my happy place,
Luna, I hope you never leave this space

The Night
by Max L. Gooch

The sun goes down
and the moon goes up
and the clouds go dark
and the wolves go (howl) oooowoow
and owls go (chant) who, who, who,
and I am going to sing this song that I am singing right now
Now I can't stay up because I have school and math!
I do not want school.
I only want to sleep in my bed tonight.
Right now I said right now.
But I'll get in trouble tonight.

Spring
by Zerek Rising

Springtime is the best.
It is very colorful.
Things start to turn green.

Birds
by Owen Dowell

Birds in the air sing
Birds flying every which way
Birds wake up people

Winter Days
by Ashley Carrier

Ice freezes my hands
The temperature is freezing
Ice is all over

I Am a Diamond In the Rough
by Nicole Morgan

I am a diamond in the rough.
I wonder if I stand out.
I hear compliments.
I see rejections.
I think I stand in.
I am a diamond in the rough.
I pretend I am telling my story.
I feel all emotions.
I worry that I am being judged.
I cry about being hurt.
I want to be happy.
I am a diamond in the rough.
I understand I am not a superstar.
I say nice things.
I dream of peace.
I try to stand out.
I hope I stand in.
I am a diamond in the rough.

Icy Icicles
by Eden DiBrango

Winter storms bring ice
Temperatures strip the trees bare
Cold icicles form

The Blue Dog
by Leon Shaner

I see a dog in the woods
with blue fur and grey eyes
and it was as tall as me

Mrs. Tenbrink Flies
by Mckenzie Allen

Ms. Tenbrink flies high.
She flies high and low too.
I fly very high.

He Is the Answer
by Mylee Giles

You are a work of art, so God says,
So, don't believe you aren't.
For you are His, you're His friend.
He will see you again.
If your personality is blue,
you know what to do.
Pray to God when you have lost your way.
Just pray.
Fear can stop you.
It will try to tell you what to do.
If you want to see the nation, don't have hesitation.
Go and explore, walk through that door.
If you are gray every single day, call His heart wherever you are,
and He will make you believe you can touch a star.
If you see a dove, remember His love.
We all have a free and undeserved gift called GRACE,
that helps us to FACE anything.
He calls us to love each other, so I love you sisters and bothers.

Winter Is Here!
by Paisley Rietsch

Icicles and snow
Fluffy coats 'cause it is cold
Dead grass 'cause it's cold

Easter
by Destiny Siders

Everlasting
Adore
Savior
Tomorrow is today
Eggs
Resurrection

Spring
by Reese Beardslee

The flowers bloom fast
The birds fly past really fast
I'm glad spring is back!

The Joy of Trees
by Ella Andrews

Trees are valuable for many reasons,
they give us beauty throughout the seasons.
Trees create recipes on paper
and harvest apples for the happy bakers.
Trees provide beauty in the fall
as we run and play ball.
Trees shelter us from the sun
and also make jumping in the leaves fun.
In the winter, trees give us wood
and warmth under the fire which is really good.
Leaves turn to compost which gives nutrients to the ground
and we can see flowers all summer long as we make our rounds.
You can see friends climbing trees
but be careful for the hives 'cause here comes the bees!
Trees last throughout the centuries
which create many memories.
Arbor Day is special because it gives us a chance to appreciate trees
and all that they do for you and me.

Puppies
by Madison Miller

Puppies are fluffy.
They playfully kiss your face.
They love to snuggle.

Roblox
by Ian Barrett

Roleplay games
Other fun things
Blox
Lots of cool games
Other fun super cool games
X-ray fun hospital roleplay games

Candy Corn
by Lily Thompson

I like candy corn
It's my favorite candy
Do you like it too?

My Brother Told Me Not To
by Isabella Bongiovanni

My brother told me not to play with my food
or lick a frozen pole-
But I did it anyway and now I have frostbite,
plus I lost most of my food on the floor.
Then he said, "Don't say I didn't warn you."
My brother told me not to get out of bed at night,
only if I had to go,
But I did it anyway so I could have fro-yo
and now I have a bad stomachache.
Then my brother said, "Don't say I didn't warn you."
My brother told me not to sleep with my mouth open,
but I did and now I have bugs in my teeth.
Then he said, "Don't say I didn't warn you."
My brother told me not to wear the color red,
But I did it anyway and people said I looked like a Ted!
Then my brother said, "Don't say I didn't warn you."
But now my brother says one thing every day in just one simple way,
"Even if you do something wrong, I will still love you, big sis."

Snowflake
by Olivia Berishaj

Snowflake oh snowflake
You make the best snowmen
I love you snowflake!

Kittens
by Mikey Steinke

I love soft kittens
with soft fur and cute green eyes.
They love to snuggle.

Spring
by Grace Reece

I like spring, so fun
I like running and jumping.
Spring is really fun!

I Am a Baseball Player
by Ethan Blenc

I am a baseball player.
I wonder if I'll win the championship.
I hear people in the stands.
I see my teammates.
I think I'm going to win.
I'm a baseball player.
I pretend to be in the home run derby.
I feel happy.
I worry that I'm going to lose.
I cry when I get hurt.
I want to win.
I am a baseball player.
I understand the rules.
I say, "Bring it on."
I dream of great things.
I try my best.
I hope I don't get hurt.
I am a baseball player.

Dinosaurs
by Brody Korinke

God's creations roaring
Velociraptors are slashing
Brontosaurus sleep

A Cold Winter Day
by Ava Lesperance

Walking on cold ice
Snow is falling in my face
I will eat warm soup

Swords Art Online
by Chelsea Romero

Sweet
Weird
Online
Rouge
Dreaming
Sacrificing

Arts
Reality
Taming

Odd
Night
Love
Interactive
Notes of life
Excellent

Roses
by Maliah Wilson

Some people say roses are red,
I say they're blue.
I say there are blue multi-colored too!
They smell so good
Although they can't be explained,
I just came here to say I'm glad they were made

Basketball
by Gabe Pettygrew

Ball
Always running
Same
Keep
Every
Think
Best
All
Left
Looks

The Woods
by Lina Connors

I smell fresh pine as I walk through the soothing woods
A frog jumps
The water ripples
The rain droplets dripple
The deer trot
The birds squawk
And I enjoy my lovely walk

Real Me
by Kate Waugh

I don't wear makeup.
I won't dye my hair.
If you want to be cool then just be you.
I don't wear heels or fancy skirts.
I definitely don't wear crop top shirts.
So don't copy others,
no matter what they do, just be you!

Family!
by Alex Shepherd

Family is very important, it is also very strong.
When you are with family, the time that you are with them,
should be spent very well.
Because someday, they will have to pass away.
You make very good memories with family and family is what protects you.
And no matter what they did to you, they will always still be family!
And you should be thankful for you and your family

Snow Day
by Andrew Hogan

The freezing ice storms
Icy icicles on bare trees
Snow is on the ground

Hope
by Caroline Lindsay

Hold on
On goes the hope
Please never stop having hope
Everlasting hope

When a Dog Owner Leaves:
In a Dog's Mind
by Jessica Heath

It doesn't matter the color or size
Dogs still have the same sparkle in their eyes
"Why did she leave?" the dog asks
"Did she go behind my back?"
"I don't know, let's wait and see!"
And I think, "What a surprise."
"She's been with someone twice the size of me!"

Make a Difference
by James Foltz

Oh! How I love basketball, yes basketball means everything to me.
Man how I am amazed by the crossover, spin, DUNK!
Also the run GET OUT OF MY WAY layup!
Oh how football is terrific.
Man players are amazing like Odell Beckham, Golden Tate III, and Tom Brady.
Like what they do they sack, they 50 yard pass,
and the pass spin around flip into the end zone.
There is one thing they all have in common, they all pursued their dream.
So pursue your dream to be that teacher you always wanted to be,
grow up to be a hockey player, or even start your own business.
Post yourself on YouTube, Facebook, or Instagram, and get yourself famous.
Like Michael Jordan, was he good when he started?
No! He was not he practiced, and practiced until he was the best of the best.
So when you feel depressed and want to give up
remember Michael Jordan did too, but look at him now
he is a BILLIONAIRES.
So when it gets hard, "GO BIG OR GO HOME!"
So make a difference in life, and be who you want to be!

Love
by Aster Davis

Love
funny, happy
hugging, crying, laughing
you make me smile
family

Fairy Tale
by Mathew Eagle

Fairy Tale
Interesting, Amazing
Magic use, Fighting, Emotion
Amazing in every way
Anime

Deer
by Keely Huff

Some deer are like Bambi for they are smart,
and they look both ways before they cross the road,
others just leap to see headlights
and are paralyzed in fear,
and that's exactly when you hit a deer.

Long-Lost Love
by Carley Hancock

As I stride through the meadow,
I see a glimpse of a shadow.
I turn around to see your face,
I feel my feet start to race.
To feel my heart beat again,
I finally realize how long it's been.
To open it all back up,
I seem to get stuck.
You wonder what's wrong,
So I let it go and sing the song.
Love is so much more than what it's accounted for,
I see you coming towards me.
Filled with love, filled with glee,
Nothing can stop us,
The world is on our side.
I feel you breathe in front of me,
I feel your lips touch mine.
Soft as a feather,
I love you forever.

Breezy Winter Days
by Michelle Rek

Cold winter mornings.
There is hot cocoa today.
Button up your coat!

Pupper
by Justin Isenhart

Pupper ran downstairs
As fast as he could go
But then he ran into a show
The show caught him
And he ran as fast as he could go

Amethyst Nights
by Adelina Liao

When was the last time you could look at the beautiful,
beautiful Amethyst sky?
After the smoke covered our heads,
When did you last see the beautiful gem stars?
After we toxicated the planet?

America's Revolution
by Memphis Powell

America.
We fought a battle of Bunker Hill.
The British were gonna kill.
Freedom for us.
We put up a fuss.
For all of us.
Paul Revere and his stallion.
Saw a talon of our nation's bird, the bald eagle.
We conquered Fort Ticonderoga, which made us all do the conga.
First we were weak and small.
Now we are strong and tall.
Best of all we got our freedom.
We are not slaves, we are not Britain's slaves.
We are free.
We are filled with glee.
From the Stamp Act.
To the Intolerable Acts.
These are some facts.
All of these make our nation.
These all made the revolution.

Cake!
by Fatima Bah

Fluffy and creamy,
Nice and yummy
Really nice to make,
It is cake!

Fortnite
by Christian Huynh

Fatalities
Overtake
Raid
True
Night
Infiltrate
Timeless
Endgame

Save Earth
by Alhassan Alshami

Sweet place to live
Amazing planet to be
Very special environment
Everybody should recycle

Everyone should save Earth
Active alive planet
Ready for us when we need it
Takes care of us
Home sweet home

The Beautiful Day
by Maram Babaker

I went for a drive with my car
I went too far
I ran out of fuel
That made things cool
I saw sunglasses in the car
The sun shined to my eyes and made the whole school bright
I went out of the car that made me a fool
I like it better than cool
I played outside with my friends
I liked it that way
We have to make a group, to make our soup
Then school ends and I go to the house for good

My Parents Who Disappeared
by Zahraa Asfar

Where did they go? Do they know that they left me all alone?
I thought they said I would never be solo.
But now we all know the truth. The truth of the girl who was left unknown.
When did it happen? I really don't remember anything at all!
Nobody will tell me the answer so now ...
now I am here all alone and of course unknown
Who did they go with? I can't think of anybody good!
Nobody lives near. I know basically no one is here!
Nobody would be it. Nobody, Nobody at all
What did they go in? No sign shows that they even left.
I checked everywhere ... They are nowhere. Yes Nowhere.
Why did they go!? I want to know! I was good! I always obeyed! Why just why!?
I wish they knew that I miss them more than I miss anyone.
If only they were here so they would know.
That forever I will love them and forever I will wait for them right here at home

3rd Place

Ellie Park

Morning
by Ellie Park

The cold touch of the wind
Skipping about me,
Grass rippling
Beneath my feet,
The clear, frosty scent of winter
Filling the fresh air.
The stars are bright
Like the hovering sparks
Lingering from July fireworks
Slowly fading as the night lifts,
A veil of darkness
Being pulled away
To reveal the rose-colored flush
Of morning.
And the sun
Begins to show,
Its new spun threads of gold
Peeking just above the horizon
Until the full circle of copper
Lifts its brilliant face.

2nd Place

Iman Athar

Daffodils
by Iman Athar

Daffodils are like shards of the sun that have fallen to Earth
Spreading warmth, among the days of gloom and despair
Spreading happiness, to those in need of it
Holding a priceless treasure, petals flutter around me
Bright yellow, a bit frayed around the edges
A picture of perfection

1st Place

Caroline Bahr

Caroline, who likes to be called Carol, is a prodigious reader.
She enjoys many genres of books but has a soft spot for fantasy.
She also enjoys writing, swimming, and playing piano.
Carol has a pair of bonded rabbits as pets
and enjoys spending time with them outdoors.
Her love of nature is evident in her writing,
and it is this passion which has earned her the title of
"Division Winner!"

Past, Present, Future
by Caroline Bahr

The windy moor holds my past
In the juniper and rosemary
As a breeze blows by
Skylarks grab it and fly away.
The cool forest has my present
The ash and maple trees shelter it
From the gentle rain
And deer wanting to take a nibble.
The quiet mountain hides my future
Within sparkling snow
And tall evergreen trees
With brown hawks soaring above.

Division II

Grades
6-7

Ordinary Day
by Liliana Miller

An ordinary day, an ordinary life, I've dreamt of leaving, that's all I've thought
the word is big, not big enough, my dreams are wild, not wild enough
there's more to life than strife so find the beauty in your life
the world is no end so that's where we begin

Life in Spring
by Nora Early

Spring showers create beautiful flowers, they also come from clouds with power.
When it rains it brings all sorts of things to life
like the soil, flowers, trees, and even the leaves.
Spring is beautiful, don't you think
it gets even more beautiful every time I blink.
I love the water even when it's deep, it's so calming that I could sleep.
I enjoy the animals running around, even when they're too shy to say hi.
I like the wind blowing through my hair, and through the fur of animals like bears.
I enjoy it the most when I don't need a coat, so whenever I go I can feel cool.
And that's why I love spring so much.

Campfire
by Emma Smith

As the pine wood crackled,
Smoke whispered in my ear,
Embers danced about,
The orange flames licked the sky,
The wind howled,
Like a mother wolf calling for her pups,
The wood soon started to crumble,
Like gravel in the river water,
And the flames soon start to disappear,
Like a white tail scattering from any sudden movement.

A Teacher
by Braedee Weatherman

Every day you greet us with a smile.
You are kind to each and every one of us.
You give us hope when we want to give up.
You are teaching us to be good citizens.
Every day you make us better.
We have moments when we laugh and cry (and sing).
Most superheroes save people from disasters
but our superhero sits at a desk with a red pen
and a hope in her heart that we will all grow up to be nice, kind,
and faithful young men and women.

Spring
by Courtney Zuzga

Spring!
Spring is here.
Spring is here.
Goodbye, snow.
Flowers grow.
Birds and bees.
Leaves on trees.
Hello spring.
Hello spring.

Graceful Dog
by Claudia De Leo

I see a dog noble and glee,
Gracefully skipping towards
Me.
With a skip in his step
Panting as he goes
Happily running in the field.
Passing me
He goes towards the sunset.

All About Me
by Kayla Forrest

Kayla Forrest
Weird, intelligent, quiet
Wishes to own a calico cat
Dreams of being able to openly talk about what I like
Without the fear of being made fun of
Wants to learn how to dance
Who wonders how mine and my friend's
Wattpad books get so many reads

Violence Kills
by Allyson Rose

Guns are brought out to our streets
They are taken to places;
Used for the wrong
Our friends are killed, no reason at all
The life is taken,
No fear in mind
People are scared to live their lives;
Because they think, "Will this be my last time?"

Tournaments
by Jade Smith

I walk onto the mat and meet my match,
Mouth guard in and helmet latched.
I close my eyes and shake their hands.
I look at my coach and remember my best strategies.
The ref says go.
I check my partner,
And kick them harder.
Pushing through every step,
I hear the timer blows and I'm ready for a pep,
I step off the mat and gulp ice cold water
Look at my proud dad of his daughter
Once again, step back in for a better fight
And fight with all my might.
I hear the sound of a clear point
And feel my aching joints
The final time is called. The ref grabs my sweaty hand,
Raising it high, he yells, "Winner!"
I step off the mat with a smile
I feel as if I have just ran 100 miles
And my team clapping and yelling

Losing My Best Friend
by Aaliyah Nelson

I remember when we became best friends
You'd do anything for me, you wouldn't ever want to leave
And I could never see the end
When I saw you again after many months, things were still the same
You'd still laugh at my dumb jokes, and we'd keep each other sane
One day, you didn't talk to me at all, and you spent the day with another
I wasn't jealous, I was just bothered
You opened up, telling me your problems and you weren't what you seemed
I tried to help you succeed, but you didn't even need me
You ignored me and started craving attention and pity; I couldn't give you any
You had drained everything else out of me, I tried, and I'm sorry
I was replaced by another, I didn't matter anymore; don't worry though
I wasn't jealous, I wasn't bothered
You had more in common with them, you disliked my interests
Any song I played for you, you'd be disgusted
You ended your first love, with a boy who didn't treat you right;
I was so proud of you
But a week later, you went back to him thinking,
"This is love" and "I'm completely fine"
I'm sorry I gave up on "us"
You prefer other people over me, and I'll leave you be
but, the truth is I am jealous, and I am bothered
Just remember that I won't forget when we were best friends

Feducation
by Caleb Pohlman

Roses are red, violets are violet
We are taught to just stay quiet
To live in complete silence
To avoid violence
But we don't
And what we do can't be wrote
We stress on education, but we lack the basics
And it goes back to the Feds
Lying on their beds, stamping our papers red
So we heat up, and cause a beat up
We get told a lie, we get denied
Our basic human rights
So we verbally fight, out of sight
But then we get caught in the light
So now we have to write
'Bout how we'll not fight
No food, no drinks
No talking, no sleep
The shoes on your feet
Better be neat
You don't want to look like a freak

Daily Routine
by Kristin Abla

I wake up at dawn
With a huge yawn
My eyes feel like they are being weighed on
I want to sleep all day long
I go to the table for a nice breakfast
The food is the freshest
All of it is delicious
And it's very nutritious
I throw on some clothes
I spray my perfume with the fragrance of rose
Slip on my shoes to hide my toes
Brushing my hair with the flow
I go to school
Tired and full of gloom
I feel like I'm in doom
Stressing over grades isn't the best
But I try my best without no rest
That sums up my days
Thanks for listening
This may not be interesting
But I appreciate your appearance today
Hope you all have a nice day

The First Trip To the Moon
by Dominic Gentz

There once was a kid
Who he dreamed to go on the moon,
who liked to moo
He went to the moon
And saw a cow go moo
and brought a cow home.

Starstruck
by Mya Guillermo

When I view the sky, beautiful from afar
I glimpse the heavens through the stars
The constellations never vary
Don't shift or rearrange
Likewise, my God's love for you
It won't ever change
He loves you more than words can tell
Beyond these words of mine
More than all His galaxies
Greater than space and time
He calls you His child
As brilliant as the stars
And your flaws won't change the fact
That He loves you as you are
So, when you view the great expanse above
Remember my God's unfailing love

Coach
by Erin Downey

Sometimes I can see your smile,
but the happy memory only lasts a little while.
You always pushed me to do my best and try,
I never thought I would have to say goodbye.
You were my coach for so many years,
but now my thoughts of you end in tears.
One cold dark night you had a fall,
then death reigned upon us all.
I fight to keep the demons away,
but as hard as I try, my positive thoughts stray.
Sometimes I think I can see you standing there,
memories of you are everywhere.
Your loss pains me, it hurts so much,
sadness that nothing seems to touch.
I didn't get to tell you how much you meant to me,
my strength you will always be.

All About Me
by Aubrey Schalk

Aubrey
kind, creative, smart
wishes to travel the world
Dreams of making a difference
Wants to be amazing
Who wonders if there is a better friend to have

What Is Love?
by Dakota Edens

With the snap of a finger, gone
Lightning flashes
Rain pours
Couples passing
What is Love?
Taken aback nature's beauty
Stunning
Rivers flow branches sway
What is left of,
Today?
Passing by hand in hand
How hard is love?
Running, pace getting faster
Turn around,
And you were,
Gone.

Ocean
by Skyler Wayne

Collect the smooth stones
that linger on the beach.
Launch each skipping stone
against the waves.
Liberate the pebbles
from the sandy ground.
Roll them through your fingers,
plunk them into the water.
Feel the drops of salt water
against your rosy cheek.
Visit with the jellyfish.
Match-up the sea stars.
Stroke the dolphins,
hear the seagulls.
Listen to the waves splash the surface.
Touch the sunset.

The Worst Day of My Life
by Reese Compau

It was a sad for me and my family
My dog had passed away
She was my best friend
I was never going to see her again
All that was going through my mind was
Did I spend enough time with her
I thought I was never going to be happy again

Dance Moment
by MaKenna Morgan

I have butterflies in my stomach
feeling excitement not fear
bright lights glowing in the dark
I hear many people cheer
For this moment we practiced all year
learning many new moves
Practicing two days a week
leaps, turns, and back bends
there is still more moves to seek
all of my dances are very unique
I was so excited when I walked on stage
then my music finally turned on
I did leaps, jazz squares, and back walkovers
I felt graceful like a swan
as quick as the music turned on it was gone

Creepy Little Crawlies
by Kryndon Proffitt

Creepy little crawlies, crawl around the whole world,
giving their web a little twirl.
There's something beneath my bed,
I always check under my head,
in the creeks and walls,
down the dirty halls.
I check my shoe,
.look into my boots,
something is here I know,
I'm not gonna look though.
It has 8 legs, crawls real fast,
hurting you isn't its task.
But I know it's somewhere
they're everywhere, even here.
'Cause, creepy little crawlies, crawl around the whole world,
giving their web a little twirl.

Relaxing Waves
by Ashley Landis

The warm, squishy sand,
squeezing through your toes.
You let out a relaxing sigh,
and feel how the water flows.
Pushing and pulling you
with the rhythm of the waves,
wishing you could stay here,
until the end of your days.

Holocaust
by Jacqueline Suida

Families, removed from their homes
Starved, killed, and enslaved
By a man they called insane
Young and old
Not just one person was spared
Camps and chambers kept innocent souls
This living nightmare occurred for what seemed like a million years
Some called it destruction while others saw it as persecution
Either way it was the murder of millions of people
The killings took place all through Europe
A madman's army eight million strong creating, involved in this massacre
Against poor, innocent, and blameless people
Now, freedom, opportunity, and happiness,
Goodness, love, and laughter
cheerful, excited, and proud

What To Write About?
by Brayden Presley

I could write about a show, I could write about my life.
I could write about the thoughts for this poem or even my future wife.
However, I think about what I could write.
I feel all the men in my brain working to get an idea.
I feel like I can't decide what to write about
even if the men could go into overtime.
Next thing I know, I feel like it's over.
Next day I woke up happy, with a pencil to my left, and a notebook to my right.
I go to a desk and I start brainstorming, and I got those men to get to work.
About half an hour, I felt sad and confused, all of the pages are crumpled,
I looked at the pile and without hesitation, threw them all away.
I stared at the note and saw just one page, I wanted to give up and cry
but a spark lit my heart and my brain started working.
(It doesn't matter what I write about, I've got my imagination,
and the possibilities are infinite.)

Me
by Evalynne Lawson

My name is Evalynne.
Loving,
Sarcastic,
and an animal person
wishes to own a wolf
and a bunch of snakes
Dreams of being a successful person
wants to be in bed
wonders what happens tomorrow.

Up
by Lucas DeBell

Up
I step to the plate
Hot sun setting
Pitcher winds up
I load up, ready to swing
Nerves filling my head, hot sun setting into my eyes
Pitcher throws
I swing as hard as I can
The nerves come out as I unleash my powerful swing
"Crack," the ball sails through the air like a bald eagle
I run the bases until I can't run them anymore
I stand on the podium, hot sun setting as I smile off into the cameras
1st place
Champion

Defined
by Brooke Henry

A life well-lived is not often seen
A life well-lived is like that of a bean
This life provides for others near
Its supportive stalk is where others lean
Its roots keep it steady from its fears
The days bring many thankful tears
A life well-lived is hard to find
It stands up tall, in no wish to appear
When other weeds intrude, it does not mind
It has no thorns; its bounty kind
Every day giving what it needs
As life goes on it is defined
Throughout that life it will leave its seeds
It'll leave its seeds ...
And spread more beans

My Heart Is Not There
by Verlene Smith

As I sit by the window,
My heart is not there,
As I sit by the window,
I wish I could be there.
My heart is not here,
My heart is in Paradise,
I wish I could be there.
As I sit by the window,
My heart is abounding in fields,
My heart is not here.

The Structure of a Home
by Savanah Kleinow

Inside this house
It has seen and heard all
The hardships
The heartbreaks
The holdbacks
It has also noticed
The I love yous
The go get them
The good tries
The foundation is
An invisible force called love
However if the foundation is not built correct
it can be unstable and end in abandoning that house
and leaving all the memories behind

What Is Opulence
by Gabriel Howe

What is opulence
To be wealthy
To splurge on cars and phones
To live in mansions
To have power and prestige
To stand above all other competitors
To have everyone on their knees by your feet
To have people cater to your every need
They have the best life right? Surely they are the happiest, right?
WRONG, when they finish work they sit alone in their mansions
with only maids to keep them company,
they are as poor in happiness as the homeless are in finances
but they choose to live that way, thinking every day they can buy happiness
no matter how popular or powerful you are loneliness can be inescapable

Last Day of School
by Hannah Kim

The school bell rings
Lizzie sings
The last day of school is the best
But I don't get any rest
I clear all my locker while talking
And looking at the class hallway walking
I say bye to my uniform
and fly off like a unicorn
I ride the plane
looking at the last lane
I say bye to America for camp
and sleep in the plane like a turned off lamp.

Wondering
by Grace Hylton

I spent a lot of money on that friendship.
Time, happiness, effort.
More than I would've probably wanted to.
What happened?
That same old question lingering around in my head.
We "were" best friends.
That's what people said and thought at least ...
If only I had listened to my head in the first place.
Maybe I wouldn't have been where I am now.
Wondering ... Wondering that same old question like always.
What happened?
Did I do something?
Maybe it wasn't even my fault at all ...

On the Beaches of Lake Michigan
by Alice Amstutz

Waves crash upon the shore, as seagulls sing their cry,
The sun sets in the west, waving to me goodbye,
I see the pier stand tall, proud of all it's done,
And the dancing sky grows dark, no longer filled with sun.
I feel the sand grow cold,
And the warm summer vibe grows old.
The waves quiet a bit,
And I notice silently as I sit,
That the sun has finally gone down,
And the sandcastles are washed to just a mound.
The beach has finally gone to sleep,
The waters so cold and deep,
On the beaches of Lake Michigan.

Loss
by Tyrone Mahone

My uncle who I wanna see
May you rest in peace
Until I see you again
Keep watching over us
While you fly your wings
In Heaven
Let the wind blow
Look up in the sky
See the clouds
Make me proud
As we pray
Let us say amen
Sound effects: bird sounds

My Family
by Yadira Diaz

When I think of my family
I think of red
Red is the color for love
When I see them I am always happy
My family makes me laugh
When I am at their house I smell cooking food
Sometimes we are all sad at one point, of someone passed
But then the sad on our face goes upside down
Roses are red, violets are blue, my family makes me laugh and so do you
My family makes me feel like I am in another place
When I see them I think of those who don't have a mom or dad
Or those that don't have food
It makes me cry

Inside a Dream
by Sophia Winningham

Inside this dream,
Unreal things become reality,
Like unicorns with long locks of rainbow hair
flowing in the wind as they gallop in the mountains
and rainbow fish that swim here and back in the chocolate river.
This dream has sleepy, cuddly bears and slimy slugs
that are snoozing away in their burrows and deep holes.
Inside this dream,
Live sweet thoughts but also dangerous ones,
like big, furry, and mysterious one-eyed monsters waiting for you to fall asleep.
These thoughts can't be controlled,
and some seem so real that you cry in your sleep.

Love and Above
by Monique Borti

My spirit
My soul
There are ways to get there
The best is love
Love and above
The petals fall
I twirl
I whirl
The dance is full of love
Love and above
I can hear it
My heart beats to the rhythm
It's beautiful
It's love
Love and above
The sunrise
The sunset
They're beginnings
Beginnings of love
Love and above

I Did It!
by Elise Enerson

Hands shaking, knees weak
I wrote down my answer
Only two left
I didn't know
He raised his board
And I raised mine
"Tokyo" "Honshu"
I was wrong
Points were added, prayers were said
"Elise Enerson"
I thought I lost
Looking down my face burned
"Well, at least I tried."
Disappointment filled me
"Has won the 2018 Geography Bee"
I looked up in denial
Then cheers, shouts, claps rang in my ears
shaking from the intensity
My mouth dropped open
Victory

Where I'm From
by ElliMae Spalding

I am from animal lovers,
from farmland and flowers.
I am from the woods and water.
I am part of the river,
whose currents are as deep as mine
as if they were my own.
I'm from simpletons,
From my dad's side.
I'm from alcoholics
where soberness is hard to come by.
From chlorine-stained hair.
I'm from missing the loved ones with 4 legs dearly.
I'm from a long bloodline,
where siblings don't.
From the cold Sunday pews,
with the book that guided you.
Under my bed are my keeping secrets,
the ones hard to share.
That I keep to
myself but I might share.

The Winning Goal
by Adie Arbaugh

Sweat dripping off your nose
The adrenaline of the game flowing over you
You feel the heat on your back as you run down the field
You shoot, and you score!
It's the biggest game of the season
Everyone will be there
Your nerves feel like butterflies crawling all over you
You tell yourself you will be fine and then you move on
Screeech!
The whistle blows while you are in the locker room
It's now game time
As your excitement rushes over you, you run out on the field
The coach tells you that you will play offense
You score two goals in the first half
But now you are tied
You get the ball and run down the field while everyone is cheering for you
You see the defenders running toward you and you get nervous
The coach tells you to shoot, so you do
Sure enough, it glided into the goal
You scored the winning goal and won the game

Dear Bully, You're Just Like Me
by Angel Lewis

Feelings that you're hurting
never wanting to be hurt
So who are you to take their rights away?
Who are you to take their lights away?
We're all pink inside and we all have a heart
None of us are different
so why pull apart?
do you want me to pop?
Is that why you don't stop?
You must know what goes on behind my shut door
You must know because you treat me like this
Am I a paper? Do you want me to rip?
And your constant jabbing along with my shut door
It makes me want to end my life more
But I don't, because I'm similar to you
And you're wrong, I've always been like you
Even though, I don't want to be like you
The truth is, in every single way that you say that I'm not
Dear bully, you're not alone, I've got what you've got
A shut door

Sunshine In Storm of Florida
by Emily Thorne

We awake with a regular day awaiting.
We walk with love on a happy day.
We sit and listen. Then run.
I see people fall till dead.
I see people still, till they are safe.
We cry. We run.
We never stop, till safeness appears in the distance.
We gather in the field of tragedy.
We hug each other until bones are weak.
We honor those who died.
We walk again someday at some point in life.
We will never forget the day that seventeen beautiful people,
died of one man.
Convicted of seventeen murders.
We go back to the place of the tragedy.
Where it all happened at.
We jump when a book hits the ground.
We jump when a door slams closed.
We never forget the day it all happened.
In a flick of a second.

Uncontrollable Power
by Caitlin McGivern

Adrenaline rushing through my veins
Speed, light, fear, concern
Sit back, still, eyes open
Could be my last moment on Earth
Life FLASHING before my eyes
Swerves, twists, turns, loops
Stomach twists, turns, aches again repetitively
Ups, downs, highs, lows
Happens fast then it's over.
Control, power, flat ground
Never fast, always slow
Fear, devastation
Always low, always fine
Still searching for something
You want to understand but you don't
Will never be relatable
Will never be empathetic
Ego takes control rushing through veins
Never be the same.
As the others.

A Chess Game Is Like Your Life
by Leyton Zerba

A chess game is like your life
Surprises at every corner
You don't know what will happen next
You start out fresh when you're born
With many important resources that can help you a lot
But if you're not careful they will be gone in a flash
Each turn is like a life decision
You have to think each one through
One tiny mistake can haunt you
But if a mistake is made you have to go on
Continue with the game
Not let one decision ruin your life forever
You have to move on
Over time you will start to grow thin on options
All your resources are dead
And there's just you
Your lonely king is standing there like a pillar of hope
But no hope comes so it's time for your end
You run while you can but then it's too late
Checkmate ... You're gone

My Black Rose
by Isabel Lynde

My Black Rose was blooming
Graceful and sweet
My Black Rose was looming
Around the corner of the street
She followed me home one day
She said she was bored
I said I would show her the way
And bring her to the Lord
But she was my Black Rose
Wilted and fallen
She wanted to dance upon her toes
For she knew the Rose Ballet was her calling.

When You Die
by Andrew Dodson

When you die you go to Heaven
When I get there I hope there is a 7-Eleven
I hope I don't go to the other place
because I don't want to see that space
In Heaven you live forever
It's as easy as pulling a lever
I also hope there is a Baskin-Robbins
Everyone not in Heaven will be sobbing
When you see the light go to it
Your life will be more lit
You'll have a great time
It's as easy as spending a dime

Marching Soldiers
by Shea Breeden

Here they come, marching in, like ants to a crumb
Here they come, marching in, like the cold to make you numb
Here they come, marching in, just because of their master
Here they come, marching in, like a disease, growing faster
Here they come, marching in, taking over the towns
Here they come, marching in, people screaming in their nightgowns
Here they come, marching in, getting rid of all of the stars
Here they come, marching in, crowding us like cars
Here they come, marching in, taking the stars to camp
Here they come, marching in, coming like flies to a lamp
Here they come, marching in, their symbol will forever haunt us
Here they come, marching in, the thought will forever daunt us

The King's Pets
by Hayden Sullivan

A long time ago
King's pet
He had a dog
The dog was a Wiener
And he had a Greyhound
That ate the Wiener
With mustard
And German Shepherd
That ate the Greyhound
And a Great Dane
That ate the German Shepherd

Battle Ready
by Parker Ritchey

People say I'm weak
I haven't even battled yet
You never use me, or even look at me
I only want to battle
Just once to show you my power
Use me, I'll grow stronger
Use me, I'll obey
Use me, please
Please stop saying I'm weak
I'm strong
All you have to do is find me
And use me

Seasons of the Year
by Tobias Grubbs

Flowers start blooming
Bees pollinating flowers
Baby animals
Birds chirping in trees
Trees with leaves providing shade
The sun shining bright
Leaves changing color
The colors red, orange, yellow
Falling to the floor
Snowflakes drifting down
Animals hibernating
Days getting shorter

Moving On
by Claudia Reel

Bees, they buzz
Rain, it falls
Wind, it blows
Dogs, they bark
Birds, they fly
Stars, they shine
everything has a purpose
All around you something was there for a reason
What if we lose something
We still just move on with our life
Waves, they crash
Horses, they run
Children, they cry
Tears, they dry
Cuts, they heal
Hills, they sing
Fish, they swim
But what if we take all of it away
There would be nothing on this Earth to see
How do we move on from that

Tablet
by Brian Peralta

Tablet O tabby
Tablet O tabby, where are you now
Come back to me for now I frown
Without you there is no time
To play the music really loud,
Loud and proud the music goes in my head,
so now is left not much pride
Without you I leave a sigh,
Screen so glitchy
Because of a Nerf gun
Now you are gone
I have less fun
Jumped off the bed on to the floor
then you decided to break your core
You have made a chore
To get more cash
Because of a smash
A load of money I need to fix
To get you back, rest in peace
For I get the pieces
To get you back

Living With Anxiety
by Emily Alexander

My anxiety is holding me back,
Confidence is what I lack.
My mind says you will hate me,
My brain won't let me be.
I'm scared of what others or I say,
What my actions make of me.
Whether good or bad,
I am terrified of what I might be.
In the future I say,
"I will be great someday."
But deep down inside I know
I'm not the shadow of a rainbow.
My actions and words hurt others,
When I never try to be hurtful.
I'm not perfect like others or say that I am,
I am a mess and can be called ungrateful.
I'll wrap this up,
'Cause I don't want to waste your time.
After all you are the judge,
And I shouldn't bother you with my rhyme.

Hurry and Scurry
by Kara Tompkins

Hamsters
They're furry, they scurry,
And are always in a hurry.
Noses
Perpetually twitching,
Always snitching smells.
Teeth
Gnaw a lot
Almost never stop
Growing and nibbling.
Paws
Ever-working
Ever-searching
For something to do.
Ears
Never pause
In their cause
To catch every tiny sound.
And when these creatures hurry and scurry,
In a flash, they are hidden.

Jade the Maid
by Anna Hamilton

There once was a girl named Jade
Then she became a maid
She hung the clothes
And watered the rose
But she did not get paid

Jesus Loves Us
by Ethan Bohn

I will go anywhere Jesus tells me to
I will stay with him and follow him,
Jesus is my savior
The almighty savior
We love Jesus
He loves us too.

Me
by Mabry Broadwater

Intelligent, creative, curious
Wishes to join the University of Arkansas' dance team.
Dreams of going to Paris
Wants to solve cancer
Who wonders who invented paper.

The Cookie
by Raymond Garcia

My cookies are soft, too high on the shelf
They still look quite delicious, what I say to myself
Being out of sight they were missed very much
But when I get to have them there will be a bunch
Now I'm saying it's very yummy, to everyone else.

Three Constants
by Konnor Olson

There are three constants, life, death, and God
the three constants, two materialistic, one holy and infinite
without God there is no life, without life there is no death
some constants we like better than others,
we may love life but we hate death, but the cycle has to continue
God, life, death, or there would be nothing
and always remember, after death comes God.

Bruce and Goose
by Bruce DeWulf

My name is Bruce
I sleep with a goose
with a hen
in a den
with a goose.

Bob the Frog
by Grace Gessinger

There once was a frog named Bob
He used to live on a log
He snapped his back
When he jumped on a crack
Now he can't jump at all!

Falling Into Holes
by Julia Seifer

There once was a girl named Nicole
She was always falling into holes
The dirt was rough
Getting up was tough
Because she always broke her toes

The Dog
by Kourtney Zarycki

The dog loves to run
The dog hates having fun
It hates outdoors
But still is adored
The dog hates the sun

The Girl That Was Running
by Emily Swihart

Once there was a girl that was running
She had a cat that was stunning
But then one day
they made their way
There was a girl that running

All About Me
by Hannah Davis

Shy
Smart
Caring
Wishes to get a bigger room.
Dreams of getting another brother.
Wants to go to Paris.
Who wonders what crazy things will happen next.

Dogs and Cats
by Lauren LaClair

Dogs
Fuzzy Friendly
Playing Cuddling Chewing
Most loving animals on the planet
Meowing Purring Playing
Fluffy Friendly
Cats

Halloween / Christmas
by Ethan Black

Christmas
fun, cold
opening, snowing, freezing
Christmas is fun, Halloween is scary
scaring, tricking, treating
dark, horror
Halloween

Death
by Jeremiah Carcamo

I saw death, he's big
I saw death, he's strong
I saw him trying to dig
I heard him playing a song
I saw a gate going up and down
I feel like I'm the only one in town
I tried to fight him with all my might
But in the end I just gave in to the light.

Logan
by Logan Mikel

Trustworthy
Happy
Kind
Wishes to breathe underwater
Dreams of making everybody happy
Wants to go on a hunting trip
Who wonders why grass is green

In the Sea
by Jonathan Sharath

In the sea within me is a dream.
Under the sea in my dream brings me a key,
Which I can agree or scream.
I am an absentee of the sea,
which gives me a guarantee of a key which I seek in the sea.
An attendee of the sea will adopt me,
This will reveal my dream that I need.

Turn the Page
by Gabriel Belanger

Every day goes by faster and faster
At that point does anything matter
You just need to look at the sky
Then let out a big sigh
Everything you do changes the world
You just can't lay down curled
We can't stop that we age
But we must turn the page

Friendship
by Livi Soell

Friendship is like the weather,
A daily essential part,
Sometimes it is bright when you are together,
But sometimes it can break your heart,
A relationship can be tough as leather,
But without teamwork it can easily fall apart,
You have to be strong together,
And then you will have a happy heart.

Stars Have a Story Too
by Alexa Calleja

Stars have a story
Just like you and me
They twinkle in the night sky
For all those to see
Their stories are quite different from ours
They start in the galaxy
Ablaze in mortal tranquility
An amazing sight to see
Do they dream of fairy tales?
Or do they dream at all?
Some questions are yet to be answered
Or never answered at all
I wonder if they could fly
Oh ever so high
Or if they're lonely
Like lost souls in the bright blue sea
Stars have a story
For everyone to believe

The Egg Gang
by Braden Smith

They look like the real thing
They're yellow and white
They bring relief when people feel mad
One amazing colorful egg.
They smell like egg in a frying pan.
They like to be sprinkled in pepper and salt.
They really hate cooking with bacon in the pan.
The white and the yolk never want to split apart from each other.
One amazing colorful egg.
They love to be squashed with people's hands.
They try to cheer when they see me.
They shout when they see their rival.
If they only knew that the germs that were on them.
One amazing colorful egg.
The boss of them is me.
I like to take them on adventures.
They especially like to go skydiving
They do what they want to do.

Don't Cry Sis
by Izabella Jones

Sister, I know, but please don't cry tonight
Sister, I know we been though a lot
Sister, I believe in you
We soon find Daddy I promise
Just please don't cry yourself to sleep tonight
Just stay calm tonight
Sister, me and Mom gots a plan
Just wait till then we bring him home
Just a few more days to go
Sister, today the day your birthday
Me and Mom are sorry
Daddy is home but is he good
But till then is let's go away for a little party
Now I have to break the news
Mommy and Daddy are now though
they don't like each other but I shall go away with Daddy
we must part ways like Mommy and Daddy
me and Dad, you and Mom, I shall miss you my sister

The Two Sides of Red
by Charlotte Hemmerich

Love, hate, darkness, fate
Sunset, sunrise, king of lies
A heart, a rose, then evil grows.
Consuming, deceiving, the gullible believing
That it is nothing but a means of perceiving.
The hate, the pain, fear controlling,
What can we do to stop this from happening?
The fire is cheery, the fire is bright,
The fire burns all day and night.
Burning all hope, burning the light,
But then it comes to pierce the night.
Velvet, rubies, wealth, romance,
The goodness of this world to enhance.
Knowledge wrapped up in rich red covers
Warm flames for the feet and the heart.
Oh the pain in this world, but the beauty also.
The people look at the same color and see
The two sides of red

In the Highlands; STEM School Shooting In Colorado
by Lilly Parker

All our life we've been prepared
For what to do with the gunshots out there
But when the worst is to come, we can hardly bear
To see all those young, lost faces out there
Devon and Alec, like Bonnie and Clyde, came to commit those murders inside
We pay our respects to the Highland school
Now I'm stuck here wondering, "Will it be me too?"
When will it stop?
Those murders inside
When will it stop?
They have to stop.

Open Book
by Randi Demerath

I open a book
And I vanish
In with the tale I go
I'm nowhere to be seen
As I ride on a dragon
Or go back to World War I
I opened a book
and out came an entire world
With the movement of a single finger
I go deeper into the new world
I opened a book

What Does It Mean To Be an Artist?
by Anna Lavigne

A painter, an illustrator, a doodler too;
A poet, photographer, musician, or dancer.
We all have different talents, art sets us apart.
From one way to another, we are all the same in our hearts.
Deep down inside, we are all artists in our own special way.
We paint the canvas of our lives, filling it with colors, light and dull.
An artist is us, all different in ways; we laugh, we sing, we enjoy the day.
An artist is there in hard times to bring out the light and guide you home.
An artist is special, unique.
We all have one in us, we just got to dig deep.
An artist is us, an artist is me, an artist is who you are meant to be.

Archery
by Victoria Kuznicki

Bow, arrow
Fast then slow
One arrow goes up
Another one down
On the targets
All the arrows in the center
For perfect 300
Getting first place
Now gone till next year
Hope to see you there next year

Gone
by Margaret Schott

Words are like raindrops
They fall never to be seen again
A lot of things are like that
In fact maybe everything
Everything we have now
Will be gone one day
Never to be seen or heard ever again
GONE!
GONE!
GONE!

Life
by Lilly Wilks-Case

Sad, dreary cries, deep sighs
Love, it will break your heart
Happy, sometimes you'll find it
Depressed, deep, dark places
Memories, they only last so long until you forget
Friends, some are good, some are bad
Disappointment, lots of it
Life, it's okay for most but it's not for everyone
Life will play games,
It matters if you play back

Lobster
by Olivia Sexton

In the sea there might be,
A little creature waiting to be seen.
Red, dangerous and full of fright,
This animal loves to see the light.
But as a lobster, his problem might be,
That way down deep inside the sea,
This lobster is very shy,
Won't make friends with other guys.
So if you are a lobster too,
Do not be afraid or blue.
Be yourself, you always hear,
Well I'm telling you that's true, but feared.
Always just believe in yourself,
Just tell negative energy, "Farewell."
If you ever feel alone,
No happiness, like a drone.
Don't worry, because out there is someone like you,
Someone else is a lobster too.

Gone
by Ava Elliott

It was written in the dark pale sky she was GONE
The moon was red and the stars were dark
It was cold, her body temperature decreased as her time drifted away
Stillness took over HER once vivacious personality
Friends and family gathered from near and far to say goodbye
The tears were flowing like the water raining down a waterfall
HER bones were now brittle
and HER beautiful long blonde hair was now GONE
As HER once voluptuous body was now weakened and scrawny
HER once lovely voice had gone as well
What an evil thing to have a monster chewing at you from head to toe
She was GONE and it was all cancer's fault
She had fought her last fight that day
The medications weren't enough to have HER stay
As we walked away
without HER
In that moment we realized she was actually gone
-Dedicated to my Aunt Debbie
Who died because of cancer on December 27, 2012

When You Are With Me
by Rachel Indrei

Walking down the road of life,
Will I make it through?
Not without you
Skipping down the street,
Running down the road
It might be made of gold
When you are with me
How could I survive
If you were not alive?
But you'll always be waiting
Even when I am failing you
You were there from the start
And you will be there in the end
We are unstoppable
I can feel it
We will last
I know it

Master of Verisimilitude
by Kaylee Hellman

'Twas a cold and stormy night,
That my love and I,
Proclaimed to one another, underneath this light.
But the world, it was no friend of mine,
As the cold, and stormy night,
Swept away my lover's light.
"Ye have been broken beyond measure,"
A voice came to me. "Thy love and thy life,
Was taken without strife."
"It may be as ye say, Master of Truth," I replied.
"But I do not enjoy this sooth."
I gazed out at the sea,
Wishing to just let be,
But the Master of Truth sat beside me,
And hummed an unrecognizable tune.
I hummed it with him, this unfamiliar hymn.
And it was so that, on a cold and stormy night,
I left behind my sorrow, and departed on the morrow.

Games
by Clayton Schell

Roblox
fun chat
playing gaming friending
Roblox is fun
building looting surviving
surviving build
Minecraft

My Dreams
by Braxton Rogers

Trustworthy, loyal, athletic
Wishes to fly like a plane
Dreams of flying like a plane
Wants to explore the world
Who wonders if he will get to move out of the house before his brother.

Me
by Caleb Luke

I'm Caleb Luke and I wish to be an NBA player.
I also dream of owning my own basketball court.
And someday I want to travel the world.
During school and other times, I wonder,
Why did the chicken really cross the road?

Lion and Zion
by Jad Naoum

There was a king named Zion
And a mouse named Lion
Trapped with the king.
So the mouse fled to the ring
Which was a trap by Zion and a human called Brian.

Greco-Roman Mythology
by Daniel Carfi

Odysseus was a great hero
Caesar was killed by Labero
Odysseus saved lives
Labero killed with knives
and Achilles was shot with an arrow

Friday
by Cali Honeyman

Fantastic
Relaxing
Important
Daydream
Amazing
Yearn for

Big Old Mountain
by Brody Schimpa

There once was a big old mountain
it was in the country of Great Britain
it layed and laid
until one day
rocks rolled off and fell on accountants

My Name Is Ella
by Ella Armock

Hey my name is Ella
I don't use an umbrella
I don't like trucks
I don't like ducks
Please don't call me Bella.

The Patting Black Cat
by Katelyn Hargreaves

There once was a patting black cat,
The cat certainly liked to pat.
But then the cat turned blue,
And then he said "boo-hoo!"
But the sad cat still liked to pat.

Mountains
by Bella Brillhart

Walking in the clouds
With vast mountains all around
The cold breeze blows by
Looking at the bright blue sky
Makes me wish that I could fly

Up, Up and Away!
by Alexandra Fetner

There once was a boy named Liam,
And he loved to consume helium,
One day he rose above the treetops,
He could not stop,
POP! There went Liam.

Nothing Lasts Forever
by Aubrey Norder

Nothing lasts forever,
Yet everyone fears death.
There is no reason though,
Death is natural, it's the circle of life.
Death is nothing to fear;
It gives excitement,
It gives risks,
It gives love,
It gives life.
It gives purpose.
Without death, we cannot live.
We live to die.
We die to live.
Death is human,
The trait everyone shares.
Nothing lasts forever,
So why do we fear death?

Summer Fun
by Nyah Weis

I love summer.
It is a real bummer when it is not summer.
There is no school!
We swim in the pool.
I take care of my garden, or it will harden.
We jump on the trampoline- having a ball.
Who can jump the highest out of us all?
I sit in the hammock reading a book.
While my brothers for some snacks they look.
We drink lemonade on the back porch.
My cousins, siblings, friends and I play hide and seek.
After all that playing, I feel kind of weak.
I have water fights with friends and family.
We fly kites and watch them reach great heights.
When the day is done, we look at the stars in the sky.
I let out a yawn and could not wait until dawn.
Then we will have more summer fun.

Exploration Sensation
by Landon Medcalf

Landon
loyal, hopeful, creative
Wishes to be successful in his life
Dreams of building on cars
Who wonders what lies at the center of the earth
Who wants to explore the ocean

Fall, My Favorite Season
by Jaymie Peacock

Leaves falling, loud crunching
Naked trees, pumpkin spice lattes
Instagram photoshoots
Leaf piles, fuzzy socks
Halloween
Spooky scary skeletons
Creepy crawly spiders
Bags on bags on bags of candy!
Cooler weather, football games
Hot chocolate, Thanksgiving
No School!
Tons of Food!
No more food.
Back from break
Days go by quickly

Wolf
by Ali Asfar

I stared into her stormy eyes as I stood a few feet away
Years of pain flashed before my eyes
as I watched her grieve her many losses
I surveyed what seemed to be eons of pain and sadness
Grief took over me as I gazed into endless ages of misery
Would this be me?
Is this what was meant for me?
But then the scenes switched to the birth of her cub
Happiness felt like something new
Sorrow was left behind as I reflected upon her happiest moments
She seemed to plead to me to do better
To continue my journey for pleasure
But she showed me that the pleasure should be shared
There was a new look in her eyes now
She seemed satisfied of her many years
She taught me that I should be grateful for mine, too
Then the wolf left me forever

3rd Place

Ezra Bradford

Grandpa With Cancer
by Ezra Bradford

I look down at the small, frail body with the white skin.
I watch as he puts on his glasses to read.
His voice is low but crackly.
His hair and mustache, white as snow.
His eyes, green as a jungle.
He has a blue blanket, blue like the sky on a clear day.
He is in a hospital bed with lots of machines that look scary.
There are weird cords connected to different parts of his body
that look dangerous if disconnected.
He looks weaker than a wilted flower whose last petal is about to fall.
Before he was always on his feet,
and loved going to football games with his friends.
Now he looks like he might crumble into a thousand pieces.
But he's still full of jokes and a smile for me and my brothers.
Underneath all the pain, he is still on the bright side
even while everything seems so dark around him.
He is like a sun about to set.

2nd Place

Anika Ajgaonkar

Glasses
by Anika Ajgaonkar

Glasses and you - the love-hate relationship of the century.
From the water-flecked lenses that might greet you on a rainy day,
To the constant question of "Where did I put them?"
They're the very bane of your existence.
But having your glasses off is another story.
One glance at the mirror,
and your every flaw melts away before your eyes.
The knots in your hair seem to have untangled themselves.
Your skin is clear, the blemishes vanishing into thin air.
And if you look closely,
you can see each one of your delicate eyelashes,
Usually hidden by the thick rim of your glasses.
For a moment, you see yourself.
Timid, yet tough. Hesitant, yet bold. Average, yet unique.
And sometimes, if you look close enough,
you can see a little glimmer of gold.
Of hope.
That maybe one day you'll look a little bit different.
But for now, all you can do is put your glasses back on
And have reality hit you like a
Ton of bricks.

1st Place

John Murrell

John is a devoted big brother to both his little brothers.
He runs cross-country, competes for a local swim team,
and is a member of his school's robotics club.
Obsessed with medieval history,
he loves all things having to do with knights.
In addition to poetry, John also writes essays,
and recently finished first in an essay contest
for the local "Better Future Fund."
Now, we congratulate John on another writing accolade,
being named this year's Editor's Choice Award Winner!

Editor's Choice Award

Connections
by John Murrell

Fluorescent lights scream at him,
Clothing tags stab him like needles,
Insomnia lives with him, under the same roof, like a brother, like me;
I don't understand.
"Friends" are like the Santa Claus and the Easter Bunny,
Words are either too baggy or too tight,
They evade, frustrate, and confine him;
I don't understand.
We stand in the same room;
Yet live in different worlds,
His isolation room is impenetrable;
I try to break through, I don't understand.
To connect we must plug in, charge up, escape ...
To another realm where diamond mines
And dragons exist;
In that place we speak the same language and triumph over
The dark shadow autism creates.

Division III

Grades
8-9

The Struggle
by Morgan Scott

I have flaws
That break laws,
I dig holes so deep I'm trapped,
And can't find a way to unwrap.
There's no way out- I'm stuck, no luck;
I see the light, but fight the wages of evil and good.
I could pick evil, but never should.
See, I have flaws,
But can't withdraw
From the laws.

Loved Him
by Ashley Zimmerman

You love him. For 9 years you put all your trust in him
and he is all you can think about ... dream about.
You get closer together with friendship.
You share laughter ... tears, pain, struggles, everything.
You pour your heart out to him.
And what does he do with that? He starts dating your best friend.
It's like a knife is constantly stabbing you in the heart.
You go home every night and cry yourself to sleep.
But the next day ... You put on a fake happy face and brave it all.
And then they invite you to things ... "just to be nice"
'cause you don't have yourself a man
because she stole the love of your life right from your arms.
And the pain only gets worse every day.
Finally when she dumps him, things start to finally look better.
This is your chance and you are there to comfort him.
But it's not because when you show him love he shows you hate ... anger.
His attitude toward you changes daily.
And when you think you'll never see him again,
he finally shows compassion toward you. Then he texts you.
Three months later. Saying that he wants to talk and misses you.
And you believe it all. Because you are naive.
Then after three more months of texting, things turn for the worst.
You two are constantly arguing. And you two exchange some bitter words
with each other. Things you may later regret.
And it sucks because you are losing a best friend.
A month later he texts you again. He acts like nothing was ever wrong.
It's something short and simple. And it makes you kinda cry inside.
You respond back and what does he do?
Not even have the decency to open or read the text.
So then during those last few months you have found yourself a new guy.
He kinda reminds you of your last crush. But you still really like the new boy.
Even though you very well know the same thing will probably happen again.
And when the new guy asks you why you have trust issues all can do is cry ... and
think of him. You loved him.

The Wind, Waves, and Beach
by Troy Oberhausen

The wind over the sea,
Blowing the waves,
Distracting all of us from what we couldn't see,
The glooming fear of lies,
The thought of rejection,
Unseen but not unfelt,
Felt but not corrected,
Instead, it is accepted,
The people accept rudeness,
They accept that it is a part of life,
It doesn't have to be,
Using the wind and waves to distract ourselves,
From the real problems in life,
These problems sucking out our souls like a leech,
Every single day,
Life's a beach,
At least that's what they say

A Book Adventure
by Linda Hernandez

I pick up a book and in it there is a round bumpy island
I see myself on the sea, riding the gentle waves on the boat
We put the sails up and we turn left
While we turn left, the shining sun facing the port side
we fall and the ocean picks up the girl but not me
Next thing I know I'm underwater
I see a familiar red-haired mermaid
We head over to a sunken boat
I find a mirror and all I do is look at it
Next thing I know I'm in a castle
I see a mean old wrinkly hunched lady offering an apple to a rosy-cheeked girl
The young girl lives with 7 little people
They take me to a mine and put me in a rusty old mine cart
After that I'm in a kitchen
There are talking objects all over the room
A chipped little boy teacup and a nice lady kettle serve me tea
Once I drink the tea I fall into a deep sleep
I wake up and there is a big tiger and a cute monkey staring at me
I stand up and something trips me
It's a purple, brown, and blue flying carpet!!
I have no idea where it's taking me but it's really fun
I close my book and I turn off the light
I pull my comfy warm blanket up to my waist
I love to read, it's my favorite thing in the world
"A reader lives a thousand lives before he dies"
- Quoted from George R.R. Martin

Message In a Bottle
by Madeline Mia Moose

A secret message,
An encrypted story,
A long-lost tale that ends in glory.
A pretty glass bottle filled with sand,
Nestled in the beach for you to find it with your hand ...
A treasure map,
A lost love letter,
Really not sure, what could be better!
From across the ocean or at the bottom of lake,
It would be a great surprise for you to take
How exciting the message could be,
When you find out it was written in 1903!
So, when the summer comes and the lakes are thawed,
Get your act together and toss one abroad
Talk from your heart
And the message will be ...
A picturesque vision, a true sight to see.

The Depths of Darkness
by Olivia Cooper

Sometimes there are things that bind us down and we can't escape.
Hands reaching up and pulling us farther from the known,
and closer to the unknown.
Gasping for air, something that we can never seem to successfully take.
It was all too hard to bear until we heard the words, "I love you."
Chest aching like never before, we don't know if we'll make it,
but we have to try,
because now we see the small but growing dot of light just up ahead.
Hope.
If only we could reach it, just raise an arm and drag us forward,
but the bonds hold us back.
Not knowing what we will become, but knowing that it has to be better
than this, it just has to be, we take the first step.
Hope gave us the driving force to crawl toward that light
and not let the darkness swallow us whole.
Yes, it may be unreliable, but it is the only thing we have.
Inch by inch, we crawl toward the light,
every inch breaking a bond that tied us to the dark.
We can breathe, the pain that tied us down before, fading.
We go into the light, not because we were released by the dark
but because we had our own willpower to do so.
Darkness may have pulled us down,
but we had the strength to pull us back up.
Stand strong.
Maintain your own willpower
and you won't be dragged into the depths of darkness.

I Am
by Dallas Wheaton

I am smart and nice
I wonder if a girl likes me (probably not)
I hear tick tock sounds made by a glass bottle
I see purple dots sometimes
I want a girlfriend
I am smart and nice
I pretend that I'm in a world with zombies and I have a Halo Warthog
I feel my dead dog's fur sometimes
I touch the titanium on Halo SPARTAN armor
I worry when my dad drives fast
I cry when my favorite dog died
I am smart and nice
I understand life isn't always what it's made out to be
I say I love the United States of 'Merica
I dream about video games
I try to the best I can in choir
I hope to be one of the best YouTubers down the road
I am smart and nice

Rainbow
by Alexandra McCluskey

Red
A war with fire and blood, longing and hatred.
Thrown together with the sea I become power
I am danger and strength.
Orange
Joy and warmth describe me
The core of creativity, enthusiasm
I am encouragement and change.
Yellow
The epitome of happiness and hope, purifying like fire.
Mixed with the sky I produce life,
I am clarity and energy.
Green
A forest of life and renewal, growth and harmony
Blend of happiness and the sea, a sanctuary.
Blue
A original, like the sky and sea,
Faith and trust, wisdom and confidence.
Indigo
I am powerful and dignified, devotion and justice
made up of fire and sky
I am space
Violet
I am imagination and dreams, the future
A brew of fire and the sea, like a spiritual enlightenment

Even Though
by Emily Shields

I hear your words even though
I have no ears
I speak to you even though
I have no mouth
You hear my soft whispers in the cool night breeze
You share your fears while everyone sleeps
I can feel your emotions even though
I have no heart
I share your thoughts even though
I have no brain
I feel your pain even though
I have no soul
I watch you day and night
I see you struggle and I see you fight
So I tell you now, even though
I have no eyes
That I am the all-seeing moon
In the skies.

Connection
by Rebecca Dorton

There's a lot going on, but nothing is happening
While everyone is focused on their phones and celebrities
while everything is blackening
People are crashing and burning, starving and killing because they must survive
Yet everyone focuses on small talk, like "How are you?" attempting to avoid
All we can say is "Good," but no one truly has an answer,
meanwhile, turning devoid of color
We're all fading away, they're digging into our brains
and taking away everything we once were
It's innocence, power, creativity, love and youth that they fear
All we ever wanted was to be, to feel genuine connection,
but society took what we held dear
If you saw what I saw, you'd be sad too
Whether it's religion, fame, money, or possessions that take us apart,
it's destined to happen
We're bound to our belongings, bound to the stars, bound to our wealth,
bound to God
They make us need it and use it to tear us away from each other
We claim to love God and God loves all, yet we spread so much hate,
then take cover
We aspire to be like the stars which we know nothing about but a body type
Everything is becoming darker, but in our cages, we perceive a deceiving light
We are animals to them, being trained and locked away,
taking away our will to fight
If you saw what I saw, you'd be angry too

Escape
by Isaac Dixon

I cannot seem to face all of my fears,
I feel if I am always alone,
You cannot escape the strong, deathly ghost.
I drown all of my sorrows out with beer,
I cannot seem to find the lonely tone,
I cannot seem to face all of my fears.
Across my face drops a lonely, sad tear,
I look at life like looking through a cone,
You cannot escape the strong, deathly ghost.
My life I cannot seem to clearly steer,
I cannot seem to get back in my zone,
The ones you love always hurt you the most.
The end I can easily sense is near,
I will forever, always be alone,
You cannot escape the strong, deathly ghost.
Now I see, it will finally be clear,
I sit and will now give an ugly groan,
The ones you love always hurt you the most,
You cannot escape the strong, deathly ghost.

We Are Dreamers
by Angel Granados

As we sit and wonder
we can hear the rollin' thunder
Hoping one day we can cross
But as we walk we get lost
We see multiple cars
As we walk
we think about those bars
We think what if we get caught
But we don't worry as much
As we get closer we can see those American lights
As they are so bright
We are so close but
we get caught
I don't know where my family went but I am lost
Scared thinking have they been caught
I hide behind some bushes
As I can hear the dogs barking
The night passes and I start a fire with a little spark
As I cross thinking where are my parents
As I feel the American air
I can feel a second chance
We Hispanics cross for another opportunity because
We deserve to be what we want to be because
We are dreamers

A Lot of Alliteration
by Giovanni van Grinsven

The cheesy cheesecake cured the collapsing caroler.
Adam added apples to his alarming alumni allegory.
Batman baked brownies by burning bacon.

Sorrow Sisters
by Alyssa Bird

We would have warm nights, even warmer feet
Pressed against the wet sidewalks
With rain rolling off our skin
Staring at each other,
Our eyes bright with watery smiles
And drops trickling into our mouths
Your hair used to tangle down your back
As you ran
Palms open wide
And chasing after you in the rain
Racing for you, you knowing I wasn't fast enough -
I still hear the soft sound of the wind chimes
Playing like well-worn reeds
I remember how the citrus flowers smelled with the wet earth
And I cry
Because I won't ever forget this
I promise.

Your Map
by Jessey Adams

Life, like the world, is a map
Each mountain is a victory
It has built you up and created a smile
Each valley is a loss
It has torn you down but you've learned
Each river is a tear shed
Either a calm stream from your happiest moments
Or a raging flood from your frustration and sorrow
Each tree represents a memory
Not one is the same as another
But each regret is trash that pollutes you
Ruins your victories and life lessons
Blocks your rivers and bottles the emotion inside
Tints or destroys your memories
So clean the garbage and free yourself
Let yourself live without regrets
Drop your weapons and biases
And clean up your map, your life, your world

The Old Man
by Roy Stairs, Jr.

My soul is red
my heart is black
hurry, quick
before I have a heart attack

Color
by Tyler Steele

Why do people insist
That the world
Is in
Black and white
Because it isn't, really
Just open your eyes
A little wider
Just look at the world
A little closer
See that?
The color?
Beautiful, stunning, wonderful
Color?
The world is in color.
And God forbid
You see
In black and white

Bad Memories
by Matthew Dickerson

Happiness gained by someone else is only temporary
You can't think about the woman
Or the girl from last night
Or your thoughts will be wandering
The way they always do
You just don't feel like living
And wish the trip was through
You run away like a scared animal
Past the fields where the forests lie
Made camp where I felt somewhat safe
All your thoughts rush back to you
Now you just want to explode
As you lie awake in bed
You notice the stars look very different today
As the day comes to an end
The gunshots ringing in your head
Remembering what she tried to say

Art
by Halle Williams

I paint a beautiful picture
With words,
But to you, the painting is abstract
And meaningless,
As is the intricate sculpture
To the emotionless critic.

Patriotic
by Addie Keith

We are free,
We have liberty,
We have a free country.
Our flag waves high in the sky
As we thank the ones
Who served our country.
Red, white, and blue,
These are our colors
That represent our freedom.
Bombs bursting in the air,
Flashbacks everywhere.
I cheer for the ones who died for me,
I cheer for the ones who are free,
I cheer for the U.S.A.
I cheer because I know
That I am free!

Past, Present, Future
by Jalen Allison

All natural, organic locs, braids, weave ... whatever it is,
it's mine
There's times like this when I feel the stares
It's astonishing that it is the skin tone that scares
You see, my people didn't fight for their rights,
So we could later be blinded by police lights
As a child I felt uncomfortable in my skin
"Why am I so dark?" I thought
I don't need to change anything about me
As I look around at black girls in society
They spend thousands trying to nip, tuck, and pluck
Why aren't you satisfied with what God gave you?
Stop using money to substitute for your personal glue
You
Are
Perfect

Mexico
by Jasmine Frohriep

A place where there are parties
Fresh tortillas with queso and beans
With the biggest quince dresses
And large family trees
With the love for our culture
We're as happy as can be

One World
by Yasmeen Damouni

One world, two minds
Your reality and mine
You see me as beautiful,
yet I can't understand why
My flaws are unmistakable
they're all I see
You notice my smile
admiring my beauty
I blush a little,
but I notice the gap between my teeth
You said I'm the happiest person you know
The way I laugh, how I talk, everything
If only you knew how broken I was,
the pain I feel inside
I'll never understand what you see in me
One world, two minds

Light Changes In the Night
by Meleah Newhouse

Meet the Lexingtons, the seemingly perfect family.
All of the children sleeping soundly at night.
Wonderful dinners filled with laughter and dishes of pasta.
Not one person ever starting a fight.
Whoever was to clean or cook never put up a fight.
The click of the front door being locked at night
and no rustling until there was light.
Brushing and flossing to catch the leftover pasta.
Dishes hit the wall, not filled with pasta
but with hate. They longed for the light
that used to fill the walls. A perfect family
does not exist, there is no day without night.
The click of the front door being opened at night.
The rustling of the papers that could split the family.
The children's stomachs growl longing for pasta.
But the family's light can't survive the night.

Love
by Nsima Usen

Love is a feeling from inside your heart
Love is a bonding that will never break apart
Even if someone messed up or lied
With love you'll always be by their side
Love is not a little joke
Love is a relationship that will never be broke

Pitter Pat
by Joi Jansen

Sinks clog
Water streams mud in a bog
Waves crash, rain falls
Pitter pat pitter pat
Against the dripping wall
Ice melts and drizzles down
The frosty tree trunk without a sound
Pitter pat pitter pat
Seas surge and oceans whirl
Rivers run and fountains twirl
Water everywhere
Pitter pat pitter pat
Squirting and sprinkling
Without a care!
Crystal water twinkling
Pitter pat pitter pat

Character Development
by Allison Johnson

Anxious, worried, stressed
Always have to look my best
Nervous, worried, scared
I feel trapped never cared
Smart, calm, composed
The persona I expose
But inside jittery, apprehensive, worrisome
Can I be enough, will I overcome?
Loved, wanted, cared for
I learned some people do
Listened, adored, needed
I learned some people want it too
I try to listen, love, and care
So at least someone is repaired
So no one feels like me
No one sinks to the depths of despair

Places
by Abby Wenger

School
Fun, important
Writing, reading, learning
Pen, paper, bed, family
Sleeping, eating, observing
Luxurious, cozy
Home

What Was That?
by Leanna Spencer

What was that?
That sound, the whisper.
The coldness taking over.
It's like it's following me.
Years and years go on.
No rest, running from it.
Taunting me.
The whisper, it gets louder.
Telling me to give up.
Still running, faster, faster.
If I give up they take over.
If I give in, they win.
What could take us to the breaking point?
Our own kind.
Humans.

My Bubble
by Muhammad Othman

I stay in my bubble, I don't want to leave,
People say I look shady, like I got tricks up my sleeve,
They call me a loner, they say I won't achieve,
But I've seen things they wouldn't believe,
I was the third wheel,
I tried to reach out with no appeal,
I guess it changed how I feel,
So I hid myself from what's real,
I hid in my bubble,
To avoid all the trouble,
But it seemed to come at me on the double,
Now I'm scared to climb out rubble,
I look out at the real world and I'm scared,
All the trouble looking at me, teeth bared,
It wants to grab me, if I dared,
To step out my bubble, and see how I fare

Playlist Pensivity
by Moira Carr

I sing the sounds of sadness,
To shed my stripes of sorrow.
The darkest dictions depart me,
As delight displaces dismality.
Treble transposes my troubles,
And trickles tenderness to my tenement.
Melodies mend my manner,
And mitigate my mangled mind.

A Family Legacy
by Emma Cartier

The wind wraps its chilled hands around my neck and squeezes,
but the wind cannot compare to me.
It shrieks and recoils from my fiery skin, everything I touch goes up in flames.
I am feared by all and loved by none but I am all that's left,
I hold my head high and shoot questioning glares at those whom dare ask
"What are you trying to prove?"
I stand tall and squared in a fighting stance,
my eyes sweep over everyone and everything.
Nothing is left unscathed.
My successor was fearsome,
he sought chaos and used it to ensure his family's safety.
Now I too must become fearsome,
a ball of energy waiting to explode in order to prove my dominance.
Now I hold the family legacy at the tip of my blade,
and I will carve our name into anyone who tries to break us apart.

All the Time We Have
by Ethan Bixler

The ice grows thin and thinner each day
Everyone should be a winner as long as they play
But it seems the greedy world doesn't want to work in that sort of way
People in dismay wanting to be the only one on top
But from the top there is an endless drop
Sometimes I wonder if the drop ever stops
But if it stops that means you've hit the bottom
Climbing back up is easy they say
But the real truth is there's a timer on display
The timer ticks, ticks, and ticks yet we all know its name
Death comes to everyone it's really no game
But the timer is set different for every single soul
Some get cheated when it's time for the dice to roll
The ice grows thin and thinner each day
In the life we live in do we even have a say?

Space
by Nora Cardella

Sometimes there are stars in her that like to stay
and others like to fade away
Occasionally she's a magical Black or even a mystical Blue
She probably goes on for miles
It'll probably take a while
Maybe there's no other place
Maybe,
She's space

The Power of a Looking Glass
by Isabel Rickel

I look in the mirror and hate what I see,
I look in the mirror is that really me?
From head to toe my self esteem is low
when I look down,
my face turns to a frown.
I cover up my imperfections and put on a smile,
but when I get home I cry for a while.
I cry for the things that make me ugly,
I cry for the things that show me as not lovely.
I push myself hard to reach society's demands,
I go to the gym and eat food that is bland.
Doing so will make me pretty,
then I won't feel so much pity.
I look in mirror and hate what I see,
I look in the mirror is that really me?

My Grandmother's Hands
by Jerzey Brown

Her hands are soft when I touch them with mine.
Her hands are oddly always cold when I touch them, but they're still soft.
They held me as a baby, close to her chest,
while her mouth and her vocal chords said congratulations to my parents.
Her hands grasped mine, as she lay in the hospital bed,
my ears ringing with the sound of the heart monitor for her heartbeat.
My grandmother's hands got colder.
My grandmother's hands released their grasp.
My grandmother's heart monitor slowed and came to a stop.
The doctors rushed me out of the room.
While my tears fell to the floor.
My grandmother's hands.
I miss them dearly as I remember the grasp, the firm ones, and the soft.
Even the one she didn't want the most. Her hands to fall out of mine
My grandmother's hands.

Baller
by Ethan Soik

I know a gal
She's very good
Her name is Trisha, the fantastic player
She dunks like Danny Ainge's daughter
She soars like Soaring Eagle Waterpark
She roars like a boar also like a door
She shoots like a legend on a sunny day
She will take your ankles any day

So
by Maia Hanson

It is so dark in here
Because you don't want me to hear
The things you said behind my back
Well I am going to fight back
With all my power
You said you wish
I wasn't born, well
I was born
So, sorry for being alive
But I am not going to take my life
I fought you before
But I am not going to do it anymore
I am on my last straw
So, don't bother me anymore
Because it is not going to be dark anymore

The Passion Inside
by Jocelyn Vaughan

I have this passion inside that I'm longing to share,
And the delicate thoughts inside my mind are hard to bear alone.
My tongue is straining against my lips,
And my voice is holding back an exciting knowledge.
My heart thumps like a stampede inside my chest,
And the bones in my fingers get numb.
When I'm around him, the gut inside me pushes me toward him,
But my head deceives my gut and I turn around.
This passion of mine is harder than any I've ever known,
It's the passion of love pumping through your veins,
The one that I long to have in future days.
The passion inside my body is a difficult one to explain,
But when I do, it'll be shown from the heart just how much I care,
And just how much this passion could affect my life forever.
The best way to listen to your passion is through the heart and soul alone.

Sandman
by Isabella Smith

The feeling of being forgotten
Is like the feeling of when sand is made into art
And is finally loved as sand
And not as the "beach"
But then a storm cloud hovers overhead
And washes away the masterpiece
Leaving a blank canvas
And the ones that once loved you
Now walk carelessly over you
To get to the ocean.

Stargazer
by Emma Jones

The 3 year old astronaut stares into the night sky
As the stars light his baby blue eyes
But he is still too young to wish upon the stars
The 7 year old astronaut is finally able to wish upon the stars
He turns his attention to the dark blue sky
As wonder fills his eyes
That 7 year old now has 19 year old eyes
Ready to reach for the stars
He thinks to himself as he gazes at the moonlit sky
Now 25, he starts working when the sun rises into the sky
His tired eyes
don't rest until the sky is filled with stars
The not-so-little astronaut takes flight into the star-filled sky
with amazement in his baby blue eyes

She Grew As a Person
by Taryn Daclison

The darkness reminds her of her sad tears.
The memory so dark that it gave her chills.
But now that's all gone 'cause she has no fears,
Now she is running free over the hills.
She learned to have fun with all she could see,
Her mom helped her out so she could succeed.
Her friends and family helped her to be,
She never even stopped when she did bleed.
Nothing came in her way, she was on top.
It was because she had found her own walk.
Not even once did she ever think stop.
Now she is not afraid to talk.
These lessons she learned came from her hard times.
Now she walks down the aisle with bell chimes.

American
by Lacie Gregg

This sweet land
America 'tis of thee
You show me I can be free
Provide all natural things
Stands home to many
America the beautiful
Flowers and trees make you
Home is what we call you
My America is free
With you our flag can fly free

Summer
by Braelynn Mack

Summer means
Cold drinks
And hot sand
Barbeques
And getting tan
Time with friends
I hope it never ends
Flying kites
And late, late nights
At the beach
Hot summer heat
Fireflies light up the night
It's a refreshing sight
That's what summer means to me

A Burning From a Yearning
by Adrianna Sewell

I'm in the presence of a beach, so pretty, so sweet;
I see the beautiful beach sky, but it's out of reach.
The sand, so hot is burning me down.
Even though I see the peace of the clouds,
So nice and profound.
I try my hardest to reach for the sky, but the sun burns my eyes.
The sand still hot, burning me down.
Away from the sky, below the ground.
I see the angels from the gates of Heaven; I see but can't reach.
So, I'll just cry and woe.
Well this burning sand has prepared me for one thing,
The future I see and can actually reach.
The fire of Hell;
I singe below.

The Poor Are Richer
by Arianna Jamison

The rich crave for happiness
But the poor find happiness within
Why is it that those with so much have so little?
The man living on the side of the road
Has the purest smile
The man counting his money
Has a broken heart
Joy comes out of others
Not by objects or money
You find yourself laughing around those you love
You can't buy happiness
You have to go out and find it
Not in the big things
But in the little things

Hail Thee
by Henry Mahan

Hail to thee our gleaming banner,
Which unites us against any manner.
And its red stripes like crimson, and that crimson blood,
which should be mentioned, was spilt in and over distant seas.
And its deep blues of the sea that surround the pattern of white stars.
Which helps us remember that this land is ours.
And the stripes of white pale as freshly fallen snow.
Show us justice to all and all of us justice to it.
So hail to thee the Red, White, and Blue.
Us, poor or rich, old or new, will stand up for you.

RIP
by Bonglee Oxford

It was just a normal day in the store.
Till I hear talking and my box gets picked.
We walked so far till we walked through the door.
We were going home, this day was perfect.
He opened my box and grabbed and felt me.
He widened me and put his big foot in.
Down to the courts where lots of people be.
At the end we would always ball and win.
Lots of days playing basketball like this.
Till one day I feel a pain, a big rip.
Kids called me trash and said lots of diss.
He took me off and ran home, had to dip.
It was scary, I missed my boy. I sighed.
This is the story of the way I died.

My Song
by Gabrielle Steele

You were my favorite type of song,
Soft and somber,
Thoughtful and emotional,
Everything I had ever thought I needed was inside of you.
Yet you told me you hated songs like that.
You hated yourself but you most dramatically hated me.
Me and my long flowing lines of sadness.
Me and my intricate piano melodies that could lull you into sleep.
You hated every part of me for I was just like you
And you could never love someone like that.

A Clown's Real Side
by Damien Couch

Intelligence had been cast aside.
Lost it for jests and jokes and laughs.
For my smart friend's eyes had been derived.
Herded from respect like many young calves
I was worried for notability.
To be an outcast among my peers.
They were not aware it was reality.
I was then showed mockery in my ears.
Had they not seen persona of great lies?
I wonder now had it been worth it all?
Wishing I never had sought out for jives.
So I beg please do not let me just fall.
Shall I just plead for respect from light kin?
Shall I just ignore the evil dark sin?

Love of a Cousin
by Kaitlyn Abbott

Oh, how little she was when she was born.
It was this day that nothing shined so bright.
How do you compare to someone more than a dime?
It was as though the sun looked like a ball.
She loved to have fun with family to have full care.
The trees would yell at her for being so tall.
If beauty could play sports she could only compare.
Her favorite season was always in the fall.
It's a shame how stars darken in her eyes.
She brought stuff to life but now things are gone.
When you saw her you would always try not to cry.
Everything I do is always so unpleasantly wrong.
How long has it been since I last saw a shooting star?
How she left so fast and left so many scars.

The Sun Above
by Ava Ermiger

The sun above,
Watches with kind eyes,
always there, just out of reach,
The sun above,
Sees but cannot touch,
A fire of passion for you and me,
The sun above,
Battles the moon at nightfall,
Rises every morning,
The sun above,
A lamp in the cave of darkness,
The lighthouse when lost at sea,
Hope for you and me.

Mindless Rain
by Katherine Jackson

A drizzle drips a soothing tune,
Droplets pound each sound into many a head.
With no road to go down,
The mindless drops decide to stay.
With an inviting sweep,
The droplets fly into a world of wonder.
With no road to go down,
The mindless drops decide to stay.
We all would wonder indeed,
Why such rain was needed.
With no road to go down,
The mindless drops decide to stay.

One Man
by Bryce Potts

One man stands against society
He spoke the truth and offered suggestions,
but the people acted like his head wasn't screwed on right.
Some even stated that it was offensive.
Now the man who first spoke his mind stares at nothing, left behind
Defies the unfairness of society.
"How is one suppose to have freedoms when our voice isn't heard?"
He states, "Did we not bypass the First Amendment? We the People?"
But no one can hear him on the offensive.
Only his thoughts can understand how he is right.
So, as we break our fragile minds,
We shall never know the truth of what was right
Of what the man said about society.

I Am a...
by Arianna Edgerson

I am a bird.
I like to be free.
Away from reality,
Away from distractions.
No, I am not lonely.
No, I am not sad.
I just like to be away.
It sometimes makes me glad.
It helps me relax.
It helps me unwind.
Helps me prepare,
For what the next day brings.

Blur
by Samaia Cotton

She's lost in a crowd
the world starts spinning, everything is too loud
she wants to move but she's frozen in place
slowly drifting off into space
she doesn't know what's happening to her
everything slowly turns into a blur
she tries to yell
but her throat starts to swell
she faints as her vision starts to fade
she wakes up shaking and afraid
she's finally able to let out a scream
but stops when she realizes
it was all a dream

The Moon
by Morgan Munsey

When people say it's raining,
Maybe it's actually the moon crying.
Crying from the loneliness,
And unloving emotions it feels.
For when the moon comes out,
The people of Earth hide away in their homes.
Only to come out
When the moon is making way for the sun.
Maybe all the moon needs is someone to stay with them.
To distract them from the dark side,
They resided in for so long.
This puts the idea of rain in a different perspective,
Does it not?

My Adoption
by Carissa Warnshuis

Adoption is loads of love.
Adoption is final and forever.
Adoption is being chosen.
Adoption is a purposeful plan.
Adoption is a way families are formed.

Marker Markings
by Sherena Penry

They ask me why I draw on myself
Most of the time, it's because I'm bored
But my markings always mean something
Like the notes of a chord
There are sometimes stars
Sometimes just little quotes
Sometimes semicolons
But there's always a meaning behind the marker's coats
Just last week I went around
With a semicolon on my wrist
That right there holds deep meaning
In the ink my skin had kissed
This week I think I'll do a saying
F;GHT ON, it will be
For I am fighting,
Fighting to be free

I Know I'm Free
by Madasion Maggard

I wake up every morning
I put my hand over my heart
I say the Pledge of Allegiance
Then I take a moment of silence
I wake up every morning
And thank God for all of our soldiers
Who risked their lives at war
To protect our freedoms and our borders
I wake up every morning
Look at the American flag
With its broad stripes and bright stars
Say the Pledge of Allegiance, and take a moment of silence
I wake up every morning
And because of our soldiers
Those who protect the flag and me
I know I'm free

Forever I Will Be Drug Free
by Karsen Edwards

A drug free me
Always stands tall
I sting like a bee
But never shall I fall
I have been tempted
but never gave in
My mom was 37
For her, that was the end
I didn't know what to do
We had a great bond
She meant so much to me
and now she's gone
I may have to battle
I may have to flee
But no matter the outcome
I'll still be drug free
I have battled today
I will battle tomorrow
I will flee for me
I will flee for her memory
Forever I will be drug free

Michigan
by Emma Stanley

A beauty that will entrance you,
Touch you, hold you close.
A sweet aroma of flowers captures your senses,
And animals of all kinds scampering about your feet.
Small steps on the soft dirt,
As I walk under the thick canopy of decade old statues,
Swaying in the wind.
A melody of songbirds, singing in the leaves above
And fresh dew settling down on the ferns.
Standing in the shadow of a bridge so mighty,
Stretching across the Straits of Mackinac,
At night, the lights show brightly,
Against a beautiful array of colors as day comes to a close.
Across the land, across the rivers and lakes,
The land lays awake, forever changing.
What our fathers before us saw and lived upon,
We have now inherited this grand beauty,
Wondrous and mysterious,
Extraordinary yet curious,
We call our home.
This, is the great state of Michigan

Goodbye, Past
by Kathryn Langston

Walked out the front door
As if he was never there before
Came back with her
It's all a blur
Piercing through my chest
A bullet finally at rest
Gone in a flash
Back with a crash
That's all in the past
Hopeful at last
I am finally not blind
As peace fills my mind
Hopeful for the future
So peaceful in nature
As I write my last word
I hear the chirp of a bird
As I say my last goodbye
My dog barks from nearby
Live for the future
Leave behind the past
Goodbye at last

When I Was Seven
by SoEun Park

When I was seven my mom told me
Don't be ashamed of what you want
Like the chirping birds in early spring
Desperate for warmer wind that intertwines between the branches
Like the furry golden dog wagging its tail
Craving for its owner's ball
She told me that passion is a growing and flourishing tree
That starts from a minuscule seed
A seed that comes
From an alluring photograph taken in the bustling heart of Seoul
From the vibrant splash of paint on bare canvas
From a page flipped with the sound of a fluttering fan of curiosity
From an untidy scrawl on a blank piece of meticulously lined paper
From the moment that you slip your first ballet shoes on your feet
And every time I would want to give up
and yield to my disconcerted fears and doubts of uncertainty
Like a hopeless bird in the deep snow
Like a forlorn dog who has lost its owner
My mom still whispers in my ear
Don't be ashamed of what you want
Without passion life is nothing

Canvas
by Bailey Peyton

Canvas
Bluish, raw
Grieving, haunting, waiting
Unhealed wound
Painting

Child Labor
by Ada Norcross

Child by child
Death by death
Wait, hold on, I'm losing my breath
Smoke fills my lungs as I'm trying to breathe
Is this democracy that they want us to believe
I'm only twelve, give me a break
Child labor should be illegal
My life is at stake
I'm not your object or some factory toy
I'm on a hunt for education
Like any regular boy
I haven't seen my dad in 21 days
I'm being held as a captive, abused, and enslaved
Here's my solution and I promise I don't bite
Give us liberation and justice
Quit repressing our rights

Over
by Sarah Kuhn

Excuse me if I overthink
Every time you speak, I blink
Trying to connect the dots
Trying to collect my scattered thoughts
Excuse me if I overwork
I refuse to be finished until I'm sure
If it's not perfect I'll try again
Even if trying has no end
Excuse me if I overreact
It's something I have to get past
Everything seems so much worse than it is
I guess anxiety has a few tricks
Excuse me if I'm overzealous
I tend to get a bit jealous
I know I should stay content
But I don't have anything left

When We Were Younger
by Isabell Smith

When we were younger, we had to fight for ourselves.
We had to stress and worry, for there was no one to do it for us.
We went from home to home.
We got split up in two, for no one wanted five.
We all got together as one to just get broken into four.
This time, not by law, but financial.
But when we came together,
No time was lost; we picked up where we left off.
No one can break a bond like that.

Coffee
by Chloe Gregg

My life started on the shelf in a store.
And while I was on that shelf I learned lots.
Someone reached and grabbed me. Oh yay!
Oh, where are we going? The many thoughts.
I love this long ride to my new building.
Oh, this house smells like fresh baked brownies.
The refrigerator begins to sing.
I have made so many new friends. Yay me!
I am so happy that I am now here.
Oh, now the rest of the shelf is blank.
But now I live with this feeling, fear.
For now I'm worried that I will be drank.
Now I have the fear of being thrown out.
I'm used as a bottle I'm safe no doubt.

Repudiation of the Stars
by Alanna Atendido

At dawn, you bathe in the golden hues of a forgotten star
At night, flecks of light shine
As you escape to the city and cower
Under beams of neon red and white
That filter your vision and hide the stars
Which will always be present, even when you repudiate and reject
And spend all of your time being shocked
About something you secretly already knew
Something you can never change
So you stay underneath the comfort of denial
Eventually, you miss the beauty
Of the violet and gray waves
Flowing across the gyres of the night sky
Flecked with thousands of tears

Big Plans
by Hana Everhart

She works all day and night
Sometimes getting no sleep
Wanting someone to help her through the night
Talking and dancing
Nothing changes them
All of this
Just for him.
All because
He has big plans for them.

Songbirds
by Mason Carter

Forced apart. Cast out. Abandoned. Not whole.
Bars. Bars separate us. A damned cage.
Why? Different colors? Different souls?
We are surrounded. Me? "Wealth." And you? Rage.
Hate breeds hate, and hate you feel. And longing.
Longing, that's between us. And this wide room.
We were perfect. A songbird and his wing.
Now stuck, we only meet eyes. All is gloom.
Songbirds are silent, cardinals loud. Us.
Red and gold. Disappointing, isn't it?
And life is so. I see your cage, the rust.
But, a man comes; I'm out. Rage starts a fit.
And I flew, to Rage; to Cardinal, with a clang.
They all turned, Rage calmed. And I sang.

A Cow's Journey
by Faith Taylor

I am in this such comforting warm place.
Oh no! I'm being pushed out like silk.
Now, I'm in a new world that's full of space.
I am desperate for my mother's milk.
This world that I've been born in is happy.
Being in this world is like paradise.
My mother's milk to me, is so handy.
I have such a unique blissfully life.
Playing with my friends, I love so proudly.
But, this changed when I was in a trailer.
This ride was long and incredibly bouncy.
Now I'm being pushed, I'm such a failure.
What is happening? I'm going to flee.
Oh no! A knife is coming towards me.

My Home
by Abby Schefano

Being an American means the world to me
I'm so proud to call it my home
We have the freedom to be who we want to be
And lots of beautiful places to roam
I'm glad our founding fathers
Made our Constitution strong and true
It balances the powers of government
Freedom lives in the Red, White, and Blue
So let's join together and show our love
For our country, so great and so strong
Let's not take for granted the wonderful things
That have made America so great for so long

Eyes
by Claire Mosebach

With eyes like the evening night
A kaleidoscope of color
They make my heart soar like a kite
The eyes of my dearest mother
Eyes are the window to the soul, they say
And in this case it might be true
With her eyes that are a stormy gray
Or a very conflicted blue
These eyes filled to the brim with kindness
So much so that it couldn't be lore
What a shame, though, that because of my blindness
I shut those eyes outside my door

The Mystic Forest
by Damien Jana

The night is dark,
Eerie and mysterious,
But amid the moonlight it is full of wonder,
There are noises all around you, WHOOO WHOOO,
The haunting sound of the rustling leaves swaying in the wind,
Shhhhh, Shhhhh,
Hark, what was that, crrrreeeeeaaaakkkk,
Go inside and learn the secrets of the Mystic Forest,
The forest is a place to be explored,
Once you go you're never bored,
There's a lantern and a journal on the floor,
Pick them up and head out the door,
Go forth to adventures in the Mystic Forest.

My Queen
by Andrew Wilson

I thought you were the one.
But you are not the one.
I am a King.
But I need a Queen.
I need a one that can stay by my side.
I need a one that can be my ride and die.
Need me a bad one.
Need me a Queen in my world to be really real and steady.

Relaxation On the Beach
by Karsyn Webber

Oh for every day I wish to be there,
Down by the beach staring at the ocean,
Beautiful blue waves and wind in my hair,
Sun rays shining on my suntan lotion.
The sound of waves gliding upon the shore,
The unique shells washed upon the seaside,
Vibrant flowers and palm trees I adore,
As I lie and watch the sea reach high tide.
The satisfaction of sand on my feet,
The salty scent of ocean water breeze,
The taste of my pineapple smoothie treat,
No other day will be as great as these.
I walk towards the sea, my feet do touch,
For it is the ocean I love so much

Books
by Noelle Cofrancesco

A story of uncertainty
The wonders of other worlds
Mysterious languages
The captivating stories
What is held inside, between the pages
Magic, madness, or in between
Truthful, or filled with stories
Knowledgeable, or just for fun
Like a movie running in your mind
Logic is far away in another place
Where dreams roam and thoughts are found
the stories of what we cannot see or do not believe
The magic never fades
From between the pages

Porcelain Skin
by Lily Klein

She wants to be beautiful
She wants to be perfect
She says I want porcelain skin
No mistakes, rosy cheeks
Perfect lips, perfect eyes
But she knows, she isn't pretty
She isn't beautiful
She might have had porcelain skin before
But now, it's shattered and scratched
Scuffed and stained
Ruined
And it can't be fixed

Empty: Loss
by Breyaiana Thompkins

My mind races as my heart hits the floor
I can't take it; I can't talk anymore
My head is spinning and my stomach turned
I keep forgetting the lesson I learned
It keeps on beating, beat beat beat
My face is burning, I feel the heat
My legs might shake, I could fall
I can't stand to see, I don't want to see at all
You stand and mock, you think you're funny
Tears start to fall and my nose is runny
As time continues I start to see
Exactly how much you meant to me

What We Weave
by Daniel Schapel

As I look into the dying light
I wonder what happened to this world for it to lose its light.
I wonder if people just lost sight and forgot what was right
Or if people just lost the will to fight for what they know is right.
I wonder what will happen to this world we leave.
When I look at all that we weave
I see no change, I see no light
I wonder even if a person tried to make a change would people see it as right
Or are people just blind.
I find it unlikely humankind
Has lost its sight,
I think we've all just lost the will to fight for what we know is right.

Beautiful Earth
by Darious Kyser

Earth is here to help
Earth is here to stay
If you treat it right
Earth is here to help
If not we're all going to die
Maybe not today or tomorrow but it will happen
Earth is here to help
Earth is here to stay.

Teddy Bears Life
by Nicole Hawk

I was given to a girl as a gift
She never held me while she slept at night
Thy girl always ignored me, played with her other gifts
I wish I was her light at nighttime
My girl would always walk past me at night
I felt so lonely sitting on the shelf
I was nothing to her I wasn't alright
The other toys were always picked off the shelf
I saw one by one get played with each day
She would always laugh while she played all day
But one day she grabbed me, played with me today
My girl played with me every single day
I was happy as can be
My girl and her toys all loved me

What Makes a Home
by Emma Lott

Inside my walls lives a happy family.
Memories are made every single day.
My days and nights are filled with joy, thankfully.
Because of the people I know today.
The kids, the pets, the mother and her spouse,
They make it known that they're never alone.
The walls and floors are what makes me a house,
But this family is what makes me a home.
As much as I hate to see them argue,
I stand by and watch the family fall apart.
But they make up just like they always do.
They put their fights behind them and restart.
They make mistakes, my family and their friends,
But it wouldn't be the same without them.

Time Flies
by Tristan Thompson

Time flies, just enjoy
You won't always be a boy
Deal with school, it's not that bad
Before it's gone and you are sad
You and your friends graduate
Some will even move out of state
So just relax and have fun
For your life has only just begun
Get out and play sports
Like pickup games on the courts
You'll make new friends along the way
So stop and cherish every day

In the Deep End
by Rylee Myers

I dive into the still pool,
Water envelops me like an old friend,
Relaxing me into its grip.
I open my eyes to another world,
This place is silent,
It is calm,
It is welcoming.
My lungs are begging for air,
But the water is so inviting
I want to stay longer,
However, I know I must leave,
And return to the reality of our world.

Worth
by Emily Hargett

You are worthless,
So don't try to convince yourself that
You are worth it
Every time you look in the mirror remember that
Nobody loves you
Don't ever think that
You are special
In everybody's mind, and in everybody's eyes
You are nothing
Don't let people waste their time telling you that
You are something
(Read from bottom line up)

Query To an Orange
by Lily Isaac

There are many dimples in your colorful smile.
Your skin is rough,
But you remain though
Holding all of the world's imperfections.
Bland.
Where the sun never grazed your shell,
Where you hide even though you need light.
The ground rumbles and mumbles
If your waxy skin peels back.
Sliced or even diced,
The worrisome knife always pulls back.
For the ice crackling sound
Rages on in your insides.
You have the taste of what the world wants to be
With tropical weather grazing your back.
How do you hold all the sun from the sky
From when it had all just begun
Until you wither with the falling night,
When you ever so slightly raise a smile
On your kind dimples?

Duller Blade, Deeper Pain
by Sophia Lewis

The blade that causes the most agony is the one that takes its time.
The metal running through flesh and blood,
it's sharp emotion cutting into fear itself.
It's too late to realize that a knife through the heart stops any flow
You will die. You will slow.
A hint of red will stain the floor.
You can't avoid it anymore.
You will shriek.
Moan.
Die.
Not a quick death,
just enough for you to feel your senses weaken.
A slow, miserable death.
A long and sad death.
And just before you die, your mind drowns in madness.
You try to grasp sanity.
Just as you think it could get no worse, the blade is removed.
The ebony handle gleams.
Causing ever-lasting pain, causing you to bleed out.
The keen, deadly beauty of a knife.

Empty
by Elaina Starzacher

I'm empty
Void of the typical flood of emotions
The streams of serotonin have dried up
The oceans of endorphins have eroded
The dopamine reserves have been destroyed
All that is left?
Ravines of regret and deserts of despair
How will I fill myself up again?
The pitcher I used to use to pour into myself seems to be broken
It seems to have shattered on the now rocky ground along with myself
These menial fragments utterly incapable of filling me to my previous volume
But I can try to piece myself back together and attempt to be whole again
It won't come easily or quickly or without help
And it will never be the pitcher it was before
Because upon shattering, fragments pierced my body
Drew blood and forded scars across my skin
So now when pieced back together
You can tell it had a Before, perhaps its Before was better than its Now
But that won't matter to me anymore because at least I won't be empty
Maybe not full but definitely not empty.

If the World Were To End
by Tathan Radgens

We have used up all of our time,
So much taken for granted.
We never appreciate the little things;
Until they are gone.
The earth once so pure,
Now corrupted by its inhabitants.
The very ones so gifted;
With such a place to call home.
They have once more ruined something so precious,
The universe has finally had enough,
We have made our final mistake.
All of the chances for change,
All of the hopes and dreams,
Slowly withering away to dust.
Our time has come at last.
Everything turns to the purest silence,
Darkness pours over the empty space,
Almost soothing to the point of total peace,
One wish finally granted ...
World peace.

Circles
by Riley Truog

Sometimes you feel as if you are going in circles,
Around and around you go,
Never forward, always back
Around and around you go,
Never enough, always too much,
Around and around you go,
Up, down, left or right,
Stuck in place, try as you might,
Around and around you go,
Spinning, circling, but ever still,
Around and around you go,
You have to move forward,
Gotta think forward, up and up
To the future, you'll go,
Keep progressing, changing, moving,
To the future, you'll go,
Believe in yourself, adapt and fly,
We aren't perfect but we can still change,
Jump to the sky with brand new wings
To the future, you'll go.

Expectations
by Katie Carpenter

Trying to live up to your expectations
Is walking across a frozen lake.
Every step is filled with hesitation,
I can't live solely for your sake.
I take another step; I tap the ice,
Murmuring silently, "Please don't break."
Safety seems like it's a roll of dice,
Its perfect promise seems so fake.
I squint through the snow, and I keep on going,
As I look down, my hands start to shake.
The wall of snow doesn't seem like it's slowing,
I don't know how much more I can take.
Any second the ice could give way,
The waves could engulf me; an ocean-earthquake.
The sea could drag me down, it won't delay,
It could strangle me even for one mistake.
But I'll break through the manipulation,
And I'll do whatever it takes;
To crush your expectations,
Like a piece of cake.

The Chase
by Kaci Flower

The chase begins
Running
Through dark places
To get away
I'm tired
So tired of running
But I won't stop
Not until I come to a dead end
Where I can no longer run
And I must turn around to face the beast behind me
My heart beats out of my chest
And I can hear it breathing down my neck
Why did I have to run?
I made it so angry
And everything is 10 times worse
I take a look behind me
Nothing is there
Except a mirror
Beady eyes staring straight into my soul
It sends chills down my spine

Dear Younger Me
by Mason Laney

Dear Younger Me, I wish you could see,
How wonderful life is, and how dark it can be.
When the sun beams down upon you,
Or when the darkness breaks through,
You will see what it's like to be a teen.
You will live in the light, and thrive in the good,
You will strive to be great, because you know you could.
If the goals you set will never be too extreme,
And the people you keep are worthy as you deem,
You will live life to the fullest, as you should.
Through the difficult trials and tribulations,
When your hope doesn't live up to your expectations.
Eventually, when the demons crowd your mind,
And there seems to be no hope to find,
You will realize you belong in all of creation.
So dear Younger Me, when you write this letter,
You will have matured, and know so much better,
From loved ones who gave you guidance,
To friends who hold you tightest.
And give this advice to the little ones you will eventually shelter.

Catastrophe
by Elliot Slater

Just walking the line,
Living life in a dream.
I never woke up,
Or so it did seem.
I never did wake,
Till that day in October,
But on that day,
My life did seem over.
A factor most frustrating
Came into my life
A pesky younger brother,
Who would give me much strife.
Couldn't do much about it,
My three-year-old self,
He was going to be there
The rest of my life.
But now I accept him,
My little brother.
He may annoy me,
But I guess it's now or never.

My Dear Angel
by Jennat Almosawi

My Dear Angel, when the skies are blue my love for you never fails to continue
With all of my heart I stand still waiting for you in the cold
but our memories decide that you can't show up.
When I'm feeling alone, I look up to the shining stars
hoping you'll come back down to take me to your world.
Maybe, just maybe, I can get a glimpse of you
or become an angel just like you.
No matter how much I cry, hope, dream, and wish, nothing will change.
You'll always be the difference.
After a while, I call out your name, but all I hear are the echoes of my voice,
are you even listening?
My faith in you is slowly running out, come and catch it now.
I'm looking around and all I see, is my shadow facing me.
It feels like I can break down at any moment
if I can't hear your whispers or even see you in my dreams.
Why don't you come back and be here, with me like old times?
And I still feel the pain in my veins, it really hurts like a storm inside of me.
I sit hugging my knees in a corner, crying my eyes out,
knowing you're gone now.
This world feels like it's missing something, and I know what it is,
You.

What Is a Vine?
by Clare Barger

A Vine can be anything
A small video that is trending
Or just something said among a friend
Some people say that Vines will end
And others say they will stay forever
They can be used to quote
For many situations
There are many different Vines
Used all the time
Such as,
"Roses are red
Bees like to buzz
Road work ahead?
Uh yeah, I sure hope it does!"
Now as you can see
I just quoted a Vine
There are many more Vines
That can be said
Even though some say Vines are dead,
I know they will always be there to stay

A Place I Wonder Of
by Abigail Atkinson

A place that I wonder of,
Place, one place with trees,
Tall, tall trees and bushes all around,
Not vibrant in color, but covered in white,
White, glistening ice that I could never touch
Without the cold reaching my bones,
A lake of ice-cold water,
Being warned not to walk on the ice,
Slopes of hills and animals there,
I wonder of deer and rabbits, foraging through the ice,
Digging in the snow,
Companions I do not quite know,
Images and vivid dreams,
Where did you all go?
I wonder if this place is real,
If I ever met them, or helped them,
If I ever walked through the fields of ice,
If I ever dug through or broke the ice,
Have I been down those slopes?
This is the place that I wonder of.

The Earth
by Luke Cramer

The Earth is always spinning
Around and around
Because of us, at night, it's very
Loud and Loud.
The Earth is our home and we must protect it.
Because when we are gone
The Earth will be as we left it.

Fate
by Kayin Baker

The universe is endless
It restlessly works all day and night
Deciding fate
Whether you like it or not
You have nowhere else to go
And nowhere to hide
You are its prisoner
And it decides your fate

Persona
by Marcus Lemm

Marcus
Fast, imaginative, energetic, happy
Brother of Allison
Loves music, video games, and sports
Snakes, my father, and spiders
Japan, Greece, Rome
Resident of the school
Lemm

Love
by Jada Wright

Love, Love, Love
Is shared all around the world
It is an external feeling that never fades
Love grows just like a weed growing unconditionally
Love is like gold, rare to find
But beautiful and valuable like a diamond
Love is shared with two people who are filled with passion
Love is a very strong word that shouldn't be taken for granted

Drew
by Samuel Blex

Dean drew Denny
Denny drew Dean
Does Denny draw Dean
Does Dean draw Dean

Football
by JB Hoyer

Fun and ever-changing
Hitting, Running, Catching
Football is exciting
Pigskin

Dreaming
by Jayden Thomas

When you go under, you drift into a weary place.
A place where all is calm, and all is strong.
But once you come up, you will be sad.
Because once you lived in your dream, it had all flowed into your head.

Meaning of Hunting
by Treyvan Sullivan

Hunting, a waiting game
It may take your whole day
But it is worth the wait
In a matter of time
You will have a fine time
Till you kill big buck
Unless you are hunting for ducks

When I Dream I ...
by Trinity Biggs

When I dream I can hear water flowing, waterfalls crashing on rocks,
and waters crashing on the shore.
When I dream I can touch the soft, itchy grass, bumpy roads, and smooth hair.
When I dream I can see light baby blue skies and bright green grass.
When I dream I can taste cold ice cream, warm homemade pancakes,
and soft, crunchy, warm s'mores.
When I dream I can smell fresh cut grass, colorful flowers, and fresh hot pizza.

Animal At the Zoo
by Chaz Godley

Ugh! They're back again
All they do is stare
It's creepy
They watch us jump, climb, and eat
How is that entertainment?
But I can't complain about the pay
Oh nuts, fruits, insects
But the best ...
Bananas
The glorious yellow, curved fruit
Something I've always wondered is ...
What are those miniature humans
The ones people hold
They are so ... dumb
But life here isn't bad
And just let me say this
You see some weird stuff
Just being ...
An animal at the zoo

Stars
by Jess Vernarsky

The stars hang in the night skies,
you find her story in her eyes,
her smile hides her lies,
her smile fades as she cries,
The storms rage on,
she loved them but they're gone,
she was brave but fell at dawn,
her happiness was but a con,
the weight of the world weighs her down,
she looks upon herself with a frown,
in the water, she felt she would drown,
she feels lost in her breakdown,
but ultimately, she would prevail,
she would become strong never frail,
she sends her anger to jail,
and put her sadness on sale,
this girl was forged in fire,
she was built on faith and desire,
no time was too hard or too dire,
from the pain, she would be flying higher,

Not Afraid To Fail
by Alexandra Sexton

I got knocked down that day, but I'm here to stay
I have frighteningly fallen to rock bottom with all my might
I'm not afraid to fail and I'm back on my way
In order to learn and live, I have to fall today
I am ready now for a fearsome fight
I got knocked down that day, but I'm here to stay
This time I am not astray
This time I am right
I'm not afraid to fail and I'm back on my way
Now it is time for me to be okay
Things have turned and shed some light
I got knocked down that day, but I'm here to stay
Finally I am back on top with trouble far away
After sticking to it success is in my sight
I'm not afraid to fail and I'm back on my way
In order to succeed I had to pay
Finally I have reached the height
I got knocked down that day, but I'm here to stay
I'm not afraid to fail and I'm back on my way

The Sound of Love Is Confined
by Sun Yu

The sound of love is confined
To keep the sounds at bay
No matter how lovely it was defined
I become so lovely and kind
Then I turn malicious and prey
The sound of love is confined
People wonder what goes on in my mind
But it's all crazy is what they say
No matter how lovely it was defined
I turn around to look behind
I thought he wanted to stay
The sound of love is confined
I didn't try to find
I didn't know he could play
No matter how lovely it was defined
I can't believe I was so blind
In the end I was the one who flew away
The sound of love is confined
No matter how lovely it was defined

Broken Out
by Nicholas Moua

Knowing life is broken
Knowing someone cheats on you
They may want attention
It's like we're on the edge on the mountain
In my head hearing your words
Can't shake them out
They're stuck glued, when laying on my bed
Being dead
If it's my fault, then sorry to let you down
But now I have moved on
I should have listened to my friends
Running around throwing dirt on my name
You got me thinking that you're mine
But you're not coming home with me tonight
Thinking back in the past
It's even worse now
When giving my heart to you and you gave me yours
You made it worse and make it hard on me
Thought that you're the perfect one but I made a mistake

Red Light
by Sienna Brown

There's a woman in the streetlight surrounded by reddish dark
Her body feeling numb, her body feeling stark
As she waits for a man to come and leave his mark
No father or dreams, nothing to believe
Sold into this life, her mom is the enemy
And her tears and body are its currency
No point to beg or plead
The lonely men are satisfied when she bleeds
She gives them all and everything
But they continue to feed
Some get careless and leave her to breed
A baby on the way but the world it'll never see
As the red on her legs triggers tears to the sink
Again she starts the cycle
Smoking a cigarette, sitting under the light pole
Dreading the next man to take her to bed
Knowing sooner or later she'd be left for dead
Wishing again and again for a better life as another tear rolls off her chin
And joins the others in the puddle of unwanted sin.

Everyday Struggle
by Christopher Jandernoa

Yet our spirit always yearns to be free
This life a gift that we need to live on
We have to fight the battle with thee
Everyone is only guaranteed.
Until the horizon lights from new dawn
Yet our spirit always yearns to be free
Although everyone might not agree.
This time we have will soon be gone.
We still have to fight the battle with thee
Many try, but fall like debris.
Our feelings making us all pawns.
Yet our spirit always yearns to be free
Loud is heard, our mighty jubilee
For the battle lines, newly drawn.
We still have to fight the battle with thee
To the King of Kings, we will take a knee
Whose power above, will soon come upon
Yet our spirit always yearns to be free
We still have to fight the battle with thee

This Empty Feeling
by Madelyn Nguyen

Pay attention to the lack of power,
the weakest quality of all.
How strong is my weakness?
The loud silence of my unending thoughts,
the way they eat up your mind and become your worst fear. Your nightmare.
The sound of the voices,
but they are not yours.
The way they perceive your feelings,
Are you upset by how off it is?
Does it tear you apart to see the loneliness so inaccurate?
No
See me,
The true me.
Not the me that they want me to be.
Not the me that I want me to be.
This agony you feel, however hard it tries,
Will always be useless to your true feelings.
Down, down, down into the darkest depths of a human life,
the truthfulness of a personal feeling.

WHY
by Sydney Brew

Why does life feel like torture
why does it hurt
pain is agonizing
worse than torment
it is like a brutal force pushing
pulling
Pulling ... constantly
drowning you with no water
skinning you alive
making it hard for heart to beat
Beat ... Beat ... Beat
then nothing
trapped in a forgotten world
where the echoes haunt
Your very being
you only wish to leave it behind
waters, you only want to wash away the fear
It cripples you
But. WHY

I Am
by Kaci Pritchard

I am a silly girl who loves drawing.
I wonder what my future will be like.
I hear the cries of a baby in the warm, quiet of the dark night.
I see my drawings coming to life dancing around me.
I want to know everything I can about this world.
I am a silly girl who loves drawing.
I pretend that I'm older and in college.
I feel everyone's pain throughout their life.
I touch the stars looking down at me every night.
I worry that I'm failing everyone.
I cry worrying if I'm going to fail high school.
I am a silly girl who loves drawing.
I understand that I can't have everything I want in my life.
I say that everyone should have a mind of their own
and be able to think for themselves.
I dream about being deep in the cold ocean swimming with thousands of fish.
I try to become a better student for my teachers.
I hope that I can pass high school.
I am a silly girl who loves drawing.

My Day At the Beach
by Trent Campbell

My day at the beach.
I'm prepared for fun, out in the sun.
Everyone with another, but I'm merely one.
My life's like a beach
The tides are rolling out, revealing the washed up sand.
My friends going out, no one to take my hand.
My day at the beach.
I'm so lonely, maybe not so fun.
But that is life when you are only one.
My friends at the beach.
I see my friends down the beach, but I go no further.
I stay away from them, as if they're a murderer.
My day at the beach.
I talk to my friends, as down goes the sun.
We're all back together again, the day is won.
I feel so happy, oh the joy of relief.
But then my alarm rings and I get up from my sleep.
I look around, all of my friends are gone.
I figure out that I am still the lonely one.

Drowning In My Insecurities
by Kelci Kipp

Drowning.
Forcefully receiving water.
An intolerable amount of water.
Filling up your lungs until you can't breathe, you can't speak, you can't think.
You're filling up with something, the insecurities are destructive,
My body is being filled with it all.
All this feeling of degradation, feeling of doubt, feeling of defeat.
Unable to speak, unable to beg for help, unable to get away,
The more I try,
The more I drown.
It infiltrates my body, the screams smothered by self-effacement
Inundated, solitary confinement in a setting of a gregarious ocean,
The indications are overlooked.
How do you beg for help
when there are no hands reaching in the water to save you?
I'm drowning and I can only hold my breath for so long before I fade away
To the abyss where I am abandoned.
Anxious for help.
Yet, unheard.

Addicted
by Noelle Simonelli

Crazy, insane, addicted
A broken relationship
What could've been
Addicted
Alcohol spilled
Cigarettes spread around like confetti
Syringes scattered
Tried them all
Meth, heroin, marijuana
They smile back, their twisted faces following your every move
Shifting his mind
Phone calls ending like a shipwreck
Phone calls breaking up the family
Phone calls that end in tears
Phone calls that ruin it all
Wish I could change it
For Mom, for Dad, for Grandma
For him
But I can't

The Warriors That Raised Me
by Ranyah Bullock

When I look in the mirror I can see who made me
through my eyes I can see them, the women that raised me.
Her mother gave birth to a child, a fighter
then she gave birth to me,
and passed down the fire.
I can feel the fight, the pain, the bullets that grazed you,
just so I can be comfortable and live to be greater.
Strong you are but a warrior fits better,
you fought through it all and you made me feel better.
and during the war, you left no man behind
when you see that they're down you encourage and listen,
you pick them up through the pain and finish the mission.
When I look at you now there are no visible scars,
but through the lesson you teach me I can see through it all.
My mother and grandmother
I thank you both for your service.
you will always be honored, for generations to come
we will live through your legacy,
and be a warrior at one

Untitled
by Emma Griffith

She slowly lifts out of her bed,
Her fingers gently caressing the meadow
And bathing it in a soft glow.
She rises higher,
Preparing for her day's task.
She reaches down and plucks shadows from their hiding places
Behind stones and below trees.
Animals peek out of their homes,
Eager to feel her presence,
Birds sing in delight as they soar through the air
And rabbits soak up her heat.
Soon she begins her descent,
Her farewell tears are carried by the wind
And streak the sky with brilliant yellows, reds, and pinks
Before being soaked up by clouds afar.
Finally, she sinks into her bed,
Leaving no trace of her presence behind,
As the meadow is covered in darkness,
And the shadows reign once again.

Fly High
by Jasmine Jaques

Days like this are hard
my mind is only on you
I try to think of something else
but nothing else can get through
I'm glad you're flying high now
because you were always blue
you stayed strong for us kids
so we stayed strong for you
we prayed you wouldn't leave us
but God had a plan for you
we're glad you're not suffering
but we really miss you
I know I'll see you one day
but it's not soon
There's not a day that goes by
that my mind isn't on you
I'm so glad you love me
I will always love you
- Rest in peace, Michelle Elizabeth Hendricks

The Argument
by Zach Gilmour

Ping
Pong
Ping
The ball bounces
Back and forth
Never landing anywhere
Concrete
No one ever
Scores
No one ever
Wins
Pong
Ping
Pong
The ball keeps
Bouncing
Until someone
Gives up.

Sociopath
by Loralai Millspaugh

I meet you and you think you know, you think that I am normal and just fine.
But if you knew who I truly am I would be your foe,
if you look really closely I might show a sign.
Emotions are not apparent to me, I don't feel fear, sadness, or guilt.
I do feel anger you see, it's just the way I was built.
I am not ashamed of it, it makes me smarter,
in fact I am just about the best thing to be on this Earth.
I will never be the martyr, I cannot even fathom my worth
I am warning you, don't get in my way,
something unexpected may happen to you.
You wouldn't be here to say, what happened, no one would have a clue.
It is really hard to tell the truth, just about all I say are lies.
Nobody could catch me, not even a sleuth, I'm just too wise.
It is just too easy to manipulate people,
there are too many weak minded sheep.
When I want something they can't resist, they are too feeble,
you can never separate from me, you're in too deep.
I am the person who is the most stunning, I feel nothing but wrath.
I am manipulative, I am a liar, and I am cunning, I am a sociopath.

I Am
by Caleb Bonds

I am energetic and sarcastic
I wonder about space
I hear the sounds of the school bell at three o'clock
I see others as equals
I want peace for everyone
I am energetic and sarcastic
I pretend to be good at stuff I'm not
I feel the energy of people around me
I touch the different textures of nearby things
I worry about friends and family
I cry when under a lot of stress
I am energetic and sarcastic
I understand things don't think I do
I say we are all the same
I dream about resolving something without violence
I try to make someone's day better
I hope that we can work together
I am energetic and sarcastic

Heroes Around Me
by Liam Dupre'

My hero is one of the greatest heroes out there.
She is just like Batman and Superman.
In some ways, she is different from them.
My hero doesn't have X-ray vision,
But she can see the good in everyone.
My hero doesn't have powers,
But she can change people's lives.
She does have one power that's hard to find;
She puts others before herself.
When I am sad,
She'll be there for me.
When I am frustrated,
She helps me calm down.
If there is any problem that I have,
She will always be there for me
Every superhero works hard every day
To protect the people they know and love,
So that's why I think my mom is my hero.

9/11 In My Eyes
by Camryn Curfman

It started on a normal Tuesday morning
September 11, 2001
Without a doubt we had no warning
We thought it was over but it had just begun
I made it to work
I sat down at my chair
No signs of bad seemed to lurk
Then I heard a plane in the air
I cried and I cried
There was no place to go
I really tried
But what did I know
A firefighter carried me out
This man saved my life
I heard him, he gave me a shout
He wasn't filled with any strife
I'll never forget that awful day
All I wanted to do was pray

I Am ...
by Erika Risner

I am annoying and sensitive
I wonder why you are so mean
I hear all the mean things you say
I see everything going on
I want to succeed in life
I am annoying and sensitive
I pretend all the mean things you say about me, don't bother me
I feel sad when I find out what you say about me
I touch the lives of people I care about
I worry I'll never be good enough
I cry after listening to all the harsh things you say about me
I am annoying and sensitive
I understand that some things you say are true
I say I am better than what you say I am
I dream for you to accept me one day
I try and prove I'm a good person
I hope you understand me one day
I am annoying and sensitive

Hidden Within Darkness
by Sapphire Davis

When stars decide to listen, dreams are answered
Time slows down it comes to a standstill
When you hit rock bottom,
Nowhere to go but up,
And there is no light to be found,
Together we shall walk
Hand in hand we'll make it there
Down a path where the end is unknown,
As far and long as it may take,
From your side, I shall not stray
For the darkest nights let the brightest stars shine
You are my star, and I, your darkness
And without darkness, a star cannot shine,
And just like the moon
We will last through the darkness into the light
At last, we have reached the end
But together we shall stay
Always and forever a family we have made

My Mom
by Blake Levis

My mom is my biggest fan, she is always there.
Encouraging me to be the best that I can be.
Always builds me up and never tears me down.
Nothing better than a hug from my mom
when everything in my world is turned upside down.
I can always count on my mom
to patch me up when I fall down.
Always builds me up and never tears me down.
My mom does not hesitate to go without
so, I never have to find out.
When my mom is not around
pandemonium breaks out all around.
Always builds me up and never tears me down.
My mom is there no matter what
and I can count on her to always have my back.
If you have not noticed yet
my mom is my everything.
Always builds me up and never tears me down.

Home
by Dasha Crosby

A place that acquires my comfortability is my home
because that's where I eat, sleep and lay my head at night.
I'm comfortable here because it's my own breathing space.
I'm comfortable here when my hair is messy
and when I haven't washed my face no matter who sees.
I am comfortable with feeding myself and getting liquids to drink.
I am comfortable when crying or laughing in front of any and everyone.
I am comfortable in my own home.
Having
Only
My
Environment

When Nature Seemed To Sigh
by Alessandra Pedinelli

I stumbled upon a wintry glade
One cold evening and was not dismayed
There lay a lake as if made of glass
Surrounded by a snow covered grass
The grass once green, now dressed in white
Looked cut of glass on this frozen night
It grew until it reached the wood
Where lean and stately trees now stood
They reached up to the starry night
Bathing in the moon's soft light
Their limbs stretched out to catch the snow
Cradling it gentling, high and low
And from those branches icicles dripped
Looking as if they were moonlight dipped
And subtle breeze blew gently by
And in the moment I
Thought nature seemed to hold its breath
For every frozen blade of grass and every downy flake,
Seemed to stop and shudder in its wake
And nature seemed to sigh

I Want To Stay a Child Forever
by Mileena Morris

I want to stay a child forever
where all my hopes and dreams can live together
when we become adults were suppose to live in this thing called "reality"
this is when everything you thought in your childhood becomes "fatality"
I want to stay a child forever
where my hopes are high and my future is better
when my soul's spirit is brighter
and everything I love I hold on to tighter
I want to stay a child forever
when I didn't care about what people think
when most of my problems were gone in a blink
but ... we all grow up and the thought of that stinks

I Am
by Andrew Baldwin

I am vicious, but kind
I wonder where life will take me
I hear the music at my funeral
I see a beautiful angel
I want to have a good life
I am vicious, but kind
I pretend that I'm fine
I feel distressed
I touch the heavens
I worry if I'll make it
I cry at the thought
I am vicious, but kind
I understand life ain't easy
I say I'll make it
I dream that everything will go my way
I try to keep it together
I hope for love
I am vicious, but kind

3rd Place

Alice Yang

Felicity
by Alice Yang

Every Monday, Felicity waltzes in at 7 AM, sharp
The bells' tinkles resonate in the air,
creating a fascinating effect
as her billowing dress floats through the door
I inhale the comforting scent of coffee beans which lingers about
when she leans in to plant a fluttering butterfly kiss upon my cheek
Her golden locks bounce from place to place
when she scuttles across the worn-out kitchen tiles
The dainty shoes placed upon her feet rise like a sudden breath,
kissing the ground only when gravity demanded so
And even then,
Felicity seemed to represent
the essence of an ever-graceful, ethereal figure
The coffee cup she gifts to me singes my fingers
But I do not let go
Her soft, glittering voice echoes in my head,
and I dote on every spoken word
But when I try to embrace her in my arms,
she simply slips away like running water
And her whispers fade with the ocean breeze
The sudden silence jolts me from my meandering thoughts.
I sigh, clutching at my empty coffee cup
Time trickles by slowly, and I, perched atop that crooked stool,
await for my Felicity to visit again.

2nd Place

Haleigh Walter

Dandelion
by Haleigh Walter

She was a dandelion in a field of magnificent flowers.
She loathed her very existence.
The garden had convinced her she was a weed.
She had long forgotten she was the first flower I admired as a child.
Despite the beauty I saw,
she would turn white,
she would blow away.

1st Place

Reid Bushong

It may come as a surprise
that Reid considers himself to be more of a painter than a poet.
In fact, his work has been featured in various shows
and he spends as much free time as possible
in his school's art studio, painting,
sculpting and working with ceramics.
While he considers writing poetry a hobby,
one that he picked up after moving across the country,
as a way to cope with new challenges,
Reid's talent is undeniable,
and we congratulate him on his excellent work!

Window Pains
by Reid Bushong

It was out of this window,
that I would watch for your car to come into view.
Betrayed by the opening of the roll-up garage door,
and terrified by the sounding of your entry.
For you to voice your utter disdain of my existence,
was by then an anticipated routine.
Like the panes of glass that would provide me with fair warning,
I too was transparent in your eyes.
My house of confidence and self-worth now torched,
my beams of trust colliding with the faulty foundation.
Your constant judgement,
became a leading catalyst for my growth.
The energy you drained from eradicating my optimism,
turned out to be a renewable resource.
It left me with the fuel necessary,
to finally break away from your suffocating ideals.
It was out of this window,
that I would search beyond the horizon for a better tomorrow.
This is where I learned to savor the sweet silence,
left behind by your absence.

Division IV

Grades
10-12

Music Is Beautiful Reminder (Sometimes)
by Mary Davies

Music is a beautiful reminder, music can make you feel so glad.
That you just can't help but sing, music can also make people sad.
The one song reminding you of what has passed, knowing you can't go back.
All you can do is listen and somehow you can remember how the day felt.
Then are songs that remind us that a lot has happened
and some can't be changed.
Music can help but it can also make things worse.
People use music to share what they feel and relieving some emotions.
But sometimes when it is shared
it gets pushed on to someone else with them realizing it.
Music varies and how it makes you feel,
just like people and how they handle their feelings.
Music is a beautiful reminder (sometimes),
but it can help and hurt you at the same time.

Where'd Reality Choose To Travel?
by Jenna Lehman

There's been a surplus of these emotions that tangle my heartstrings,
though only when spring comes and pricked fingertips
that bleed from bloomed flowers remind me I'm still living
Four-leaf clovers stepped on
leaving leftover luck from the magic inside stems of green
The color of greed yet there was nothing to desperately want
more than playtime as a child
Even though I don't think you've seen me use that rickety swing set in a while
Seven quarters and counting from minimum wage,
making up for the lack of goodbyes and promises I couldn't make
Stacking quarters on machines just to call my mother to apologize
I'm sorry I left this sweet childhood as early as I did
The greed came with want for escape to not completely implode who I am
Standing on the edge of darkness I can see all of my imaginary friends
Including the shadow man that used to stand
in the corner of my room when I was seven too
Rocks thrown and not echo back into the face of somebody
who's been inspired too many times to actually wait
So I dive into a pool of heavenly memories before it all escapes
And I become who I am, still struggling to remember who I used to be
When the inner child inside got pulverized
by these emotions you still don't know to this day
Or understand as something that's genuinely affected me
Standing on the edge I'll call my mother once more
To apologize for jumping off too early, because of her
This sorry carving tears out of green eyes but necessary to say to a mother
that left the last time that I actually wanted to say goodbye without fear
When my need for playtime turned into the greed
of wanting my mom back at only seven

Papa
by Lynlee Kyle

How sweet his words were,
How warm and soft his rough hands were truly,
His heart was one of gold, for he loved with a great passion,
Eyes as bright as the stars themselves,
Too great for a cruel world like this.
Voice as soft as velvet,
Yet a rough voice that could cut through glass,
How his words may seem hard, but actually soft,
Loving with his whole being, rather than just his heart,
Too caring of a person for his own good.
A smile that made the whole world stop in its tracks,
The personality of a kindred soul,
A joking manner that lessened up the hurt,
Taking care of others before himself,
Too wonderful for just one being.
Always in my heart,
Never too far from my mind,
May be gone from the Earth itself,
But never gone from my life,
I truly miss you, Papa.

Forever Young
by Sofia Jacobus

An old box is seen out of the corner of her eyes
Her brows furrow
The top is removed to reveal her life souvenirs
A delicate chain with her maiden initials engraved in gold,
a Vermont postcard dated 1932
Beneath all the odds and ends of her young self she uncovers a photo
She is greeted with a familiar pair of eyes,
her wrinkled fingers run over his faded face
A young man with a perfect complexion
The echo of memories fill her mind
From riding on the handlebars of the bicycle because he couldn't afford a car
Or dancing on the porch past her bedtime
To the time she took that photo to place by her bed as she waited
She didn't know at the time, but she'd always miss him
Though she'd rather miss him while he was at his 9 to 5 job
Not because he might never come home
She wanted to miss her alone time
because they would spend every second with each other
But, she'll miss him forever
Through misty eyes she saw his smile still said, "I'll see you soon"
Stuck forever with a sunbeam lighting his face, and a lipstick-stained cheek
Stuck forever in his uniform
A man who was now stuck forever young in this photo

An Unforgiven Apology
by Tyler Shibinski

Unwilling apology from a friend who said to me
He said a thing that he regrets
he tried to apologize to be a friend to me
In my darkest hour, in time I knew
When I felt like I had a heart of stone
And the rain fell from the sky
when depression was my worst friend
and my best enemy
I wanted to climb to the roof to see if I could fly
So that was the near attempt to die
That was the sadder time in my life
I felt sorrow for a fallen family member
When I felt the breath of death on my neck
I thought it was the end of me that was to be
But then I saw a flash of light
The golden light spoke word
After that my sadness was less and I felt
As though my life was going to change
And I did not want to die, I forgave those words
That hurt me, I was ready to live

Ice In My Veins, Fire In Your Heart
by Logan White

The last time I held your hand it was cold cold cold
The soft flurries of snow embraced the air
and even they found it so cold, they turned to ice.
The ground outside my house was frozen, the last time I held your hand.
Leaves were encased in ice, and I felt like my bones were too.
I held your hand the entire night
because warmth clung to you like a second skin,
it felt like you were taking my heat and making it your own.
I was cold cold cold,
the coldest I've ever been
and just to remember what warmth was
I held your hand.
We had been inside for over an hour, and my hands were still ice
and your hands were still fire so I kept clinging to you.
That night, I held your hand more than I did anything else.
Your warmth couldn't seep past my fingers, the rest of me was still frozen,
but the hand that was holding yours wasn't cold. Not at all.
I got home that night, and the biting cold followed me,
but your hand didn't,
leaving me with snow on my skin and ice in my veins,
Forever missing your heat.
Maybe people like me live icebound
So people like you can hold fire in your hearts.

Sunflower
by Jordan Cooper

Beautiful as a rose, my heart has Arose again,
barely know of this flower yet the thoughts of you bloom within,
Putting aside of what my eye and mind have perceived. But I wish to Understand.
If only you'd let me in, give me chance to earn to learn you
and witness your full potential, potentially falling within Quick Love.
For Love is quicksand to this heart of mine ... I do not know you.
Yet your beauty shines and smile twines my search for both Loving and Timing,
Creating only a Glimpse of my Peace of Mind.
With the beauty of a watered Rose kissed by sun's warmth
grown on Heaven's richest dirt ...
You yet still lose the idea of "feeling Pretty"
as if beauty and confidence blow away like dandelions
Do the choices he made still bring you pain and heartache?
The thought of you crying brings me sorrow.
In a dream I wished upon a dandelion to have the ability to let go of my pain
as my past blows away like the white floaties.
I wish the same amongst you, I know it's hard. It takes time and virtue.
My thoughts are as Grey as the thoughts that you've cried from, if not darker.
We have the same pain, I guess my eyes just haven't rained yet.
But my cloud is getting darker in need of light, in hopes that's you.
Love.

Costly Actions
by Abby Barnes

Knives are about three dollars, guns are about a hundred dollars,
rope is about ten dollars
Your words can bruise the hearts of the kind
Your words can blind those who used to see the most vibrant colors
Your fist can cause mothers to stay up late at night
wondering if their child actually ran into that pole at school
Your fist can cause yet another sad prayer request at church
Coffins are about a thousand dollars, flowers are about eighty dollars,
tissues are about two dollars
Depression is something you make fun of?
Suicide is something you laugh about?
It's all fun and games until you come back the next day and your victim doesn't
You say you can relate when the hardest thing in your life right now
is that you lost the game last night
Okay, you may have struggle, you may have pain and you may have problems
But why is that an excuse to make others feel the need to leave this world
To put that blade to their wrist, that gun to their head,
or that rope around their neck
To make mothers put their babies in coffins,
fathers to get flowers, and friends get tissue
Your actions can be very expensive
Make sure you're not making other people pay the price

Ode To Love
by Trinity Sickles

Oh love what would I do without you?
You create so much happiness
And you too
Will bring sadness
Love comes in so many forms that we accept will do
Such as loving an abusive mother to
Falling in love with a promise
We count on you to always be true
And we become desperate and hopeless
While we wait for our one night stand to come through
But with you we fall for a few
And when we fall, we become clueless
While we start to decrease our value
Oh love you are so risky and dangerous
You become as comfortable as an old shoe
Then you break us and we try to find a way to have a redo
And the ways you come are so mysterious
But when we think we have you, we fight to hold on to you
Until you hurt us so bad we become painless
Oh love you are so special with the ways you work
but we will always need you.

Who Am I?
by Ashlyn Restovic

I look in the mirror and I begin to wonder,
of the things that often make me plunder.
I build myself up to be knocked back down.
I wonder if there is a way out.
There are many people that say I am great.
But all I can feel around me is hate.
Oh, please just tell me what's true.
How I wish that I knew.
Because the hate that some people give,
I wonder if they had motive?
Let's see, did I do something wrong?
I guess I just have to be strong.
Because people will hate and they will judge,
but I will not hold a grudge.
For all is okay with me.
I like who I have come to be.
Yes, there are days that I feel small,
but I know that I should not worry at all.
So, when the glass deceives you,
do not let it make you feel blue.
There is no need to be stressed,
for you are extremely blessed.

To You
by Morgan Laney

This is a letter to you.
A letter because I now know better.
Better- because of you.
This is a message to you.
A message even though you can't hear me.
For you this may not even be a memory,
But for me it is reality.
Reality- because of you.
This is an address to you.
An address to fill the darkening void. For darkness is where you hid.
To attack.
So now I look over my shoulder,
Paranoid of your boulder.
Paranoid- because of you.
This is a poem to you.
A poem to show you how I feel.
How you affected me and took my security.
You showed me reality.
I am now stronger.
I now know what to do.
Stronger- because of you.

Should This Poem Be Picked
by Kamille Oweis

Externally, a blessing,
Internally, a curse:
Ambition.
After reading the awarded poems of "Futures" last year, my submission looked
Inadequate.
"Their poems are better than mine'; "they are better than me".
Likely, if you are reading this (that is, should this poem be picked),
You yourself submitted a poem to this contest.
Yes, you, the person reading this,
whose eyes have graced these lines of mediocre words,
I would like to say to you:
You are enough; don't be like me,
Chasing the top rung of an infinite ladder.
You don't need, I'm learning,
to earn things with your talent to prove that your talent exists.
God has blessed you with the gifts that you possess;
That is not sufficient reason to obsess
Over all that you could acquire,
The approval, the people by whom you'd be admired,
God created you, a human BEing; it's okay to just be and not do.
You are enough.
Will you remember that, please?

Stars
by Alaina Wittum

Wishing for her embrace
Or just once last chance
To see her face
To see her smile
To hear her laugh
She always had a way with words
A way to make you feel important
A way to make you feel heard
Her hugs were warm like the sun
And her eyes as gentle as can be
To see you suffer broke my soul
Endless tears and sleepless nights with Mom crying behind shut doors
You started to lose that shine in your eyes
As things got harder you left, started to leave your memory behind
But you never forgot me or the important people in your family
But towards the end it was rough and I know your frail body had enough
It broke my heart to see you go but when I look up into these stars
I imagine you celebrating, dancing and singing once again
with loved ones you lost
I know you are happy although you are not with me
But at least I know you are free and finally as healthy as can be

A Girl In an Armor of Concrete
by Madilynn Clark

I am a girl wearing armor of concrete.
I wonder if someone will ever break through that armor and find me ...
the real me.
I hear people calling, shouting, yelling for me,
but I just stay in my armor ... alone.
I see people trying to break through ... people trying to get to me
I want someone to break through and find the real me.
I pretend to not wear armor ... I pretend to let people in.
I feel as if no one will ever truly find me.
I touch the armor around me ... questioning if I should take it off.
I worry that if I do life will never be the same.
I cry because I do want to let people in, but my heart isn't so sure.
I am a girl wearing armor of concrete.
I understand it's not good to keep this armor
shielding me from the rest of the world.
I say that people are kind natured and understanding,
but that's not always true.
I dream someone will take the time to break through my armor
and see me ... the real me.
I try to let down my defenses and show who I am.
I hope someone will finally claw their way in.
I am a girl wearing armor of concrete.

American Integrity
by Jayce Reath

"American Integrity," something to strive for.
You left me, when I was only a baby.
I guess I just wasn't good enough.
And you were so big and tough.
I was small and scrawny,
No choice, but to accept what was put in front of me.
You got what you desired.
Maybe you didn't know we would get hurt,
or maybe we just weren't your concern.
I shed tears from the wounds you left, scars are now forever on my heart.
When you decided to leave, I didn't know what that had meant.
Although you are not dead, there is little difference inside of my head.
Your "American Integrity" has meant nothing to me.
You're supposed to be a soldier,
But you weren't there,
You were the one pulling the trigger, causing the destruction.
I'm almost glad you're gone,
I don't have to go see you, not like you wanted me too.
I'm fine, if you wanted to know.
So now you can go,
Go be happy with your new family.

World's Greatest Singer
by Andrea Robinson

I am the world's greatest singer!
I have control over
All of the music in the world!
I get to judge all
Of the new artists
And bands
If I don't like your music
You don't get to play for others.
When I'm listening to music,
I feel my heart and soul immediately become
One with the music
Their voice becomes mine!
I become Andy Black, Ivan Moody, and Iggy Azalea!
But, when I look at myself in the mirror
I see myself for what I truly am
I am not Andy Black, lead singer of one of the best bands in the world
Emo Trinity, Black Veil Brides
I am Andrea Robinson
A 17 year old high school student
And I am not the world's greatest singer
I am ... a bag of trash ... someone not as great as
Andy Black, Chester Bennington, or Mike Shinoda.

Umbrella
by Olivia Camara

So much depends upon
The big yellow umbrella
Dripping with sweet rain
Sheltering the innocent child
Beneath its yellow wings
- Inspired by "The Red Wheelbarrow" by William Carlos Williams

My Vow To You
by Alexis Smith

My love for you is so deep,
That all I do is think,
About how you sweep me away,
Every single day.
To the sparkle in your eye,
And the smile that makes me cry,
I love you now and forever
As long as we're together.
Although you may be tall,
I will still forever always fall,
In love with the man,
That makes me a part of his future plan.
From now and forever,
I will stay true,
To the one I love most,
Which will always be you.

The Pain
by Lorah Chudy

Somehow it's the pain that keeps me going
Whether it's the red from my wrist that's flowing
Or the pain from my binder that's so tight I can barely breathe
The pain somehow keeps me from joining those beneath
The earth that everybody walks so lightly
When everything painful in this world keeps me hanging on so tightly
I don't know when it all started to disappear
Maybe it's when people decided that they couldn't be near
Or maybe it was when I put on the tie
And suddenly it all became a lie
Just to keep from ending it all
I suddenly hear a loud call
And I think this is the end for me
And then I start to see
That all this pain that I put myself through
Is just to hide from the scars that were left by you

Unfinished
by Cody Maxwell

Close as can be and yet far away
Always tomorrow
Never today
A time when history is before us
Thoughts that may implore us
Never again never to start
The time, the day it was torn apart

Tomorrow's Regrets
by Michelle Thomas

Yesterday's faces
Are gone again
Waiting for tomorrow
As our minds try to remember those ...
Unrememberable memories!
Trying to remember the good times
But ...
All we remember are the bad
Time is ending ...
We rush to day our last good-byes
telling other how much
they mean to us and ...
how much we love them
that death is the only thing ...
that can separate us

Her
by Abby Zeller

He'd said he left her,
That he'd left her for us.
But he'd always come home late,
The smell of her on his breath.
His thoughts clouded by her,
He fought for her.
Waging a war of hurt and pain
Against our mother.
We'd always hide,
Afraid of him and what he might do.
Our mother gave him a choice:
Us or her.
After years of fighting,
He gave in to her
He chose her over us,
He chose alcohol.

My Midnight Thoughts
by Mia Talburt

I fall into the quicksand
like an hourglass waiting to be turned.
Waves of the ocean felt almost inviting
as I was waiting for the host to answer the door,
I am alone.
Alone as your first summer midnight cigarette.
You breathe me in thinking I am summer,
yet, I am fall.

Time Running Out
by Natasha Lambert

The clock is fear.
Every year it goes up by one.
Kids become teenagers then adults.
Adults are growing old.
Losing pets because of age.
Loved ones leaving life behind.
Running out of time to do things.
Not enough time with loved ones.
Bones are growing old.
In too much pain to do anything.
Not strong enough to get out of bed.
Everyone coming to say goodbye.
Seeing them one last time.
Time is running out fast.
Not ready for the clock to run out of time.

Deep Down
by Richelle Noeske

Deep down under the broken glass is a bright new bottle,
Behind all your tears is a deep blue sea, that's waiting to be seen,
Behind your sadness is a strong, hopeful, beautiful face,
The further you go in the blue ocean, the darker it gets,
but you still somehow manage to shine bright.
Behind the insufferable battles, lies a deep passion that will wake the heart,
Down under your heart is slowly healing,
fight the urge to lose more broken pieces,
Down under your tears, I can still see you shining,
Don't let the darkness steal your light.
Don't let the demons rip away your angel wings,
Your light shines brighter the harder you fight,
You need to show the demons that you're not gonna lose
in this battle that you were chosen to fight in,
Win this battle, win, to win back the strength of your angel wings.

Things You See At the Zoo
by Martha Tibai

There are lots of animals you see.
Like lions, tigers and a silly monkey.
They lock them up with a key.
So that they are as safe as they will ever be
Zebras and birds are cute, maybe.
Gorillas and bears are strong to me.
But my favorite of all to see
Is a chimpanzee!

I Need Space
by Sabine R. Weaver

"I need space"
The words no longer held by gravity fell from his lips
Space from what?
The light-years of distance that had grown between us?
Or did you mean the excitement of exploring,
The adrenaline of seeing other stars.
Seeing other moons and suns to light up your world.
"I need space"
But darling, I can't give you any more,
Our stars never aligned,
And our universe declined.
All I've given is space
Because that's what you needed.
But now, you've taken up all my air,
And I am left with an empty atmosphere.

Mind
by Anastasia LaBonte

The mind is an overtaking place,
Lets you dream while you're awake
It can be sweeter than a strawberry milkshake,
But as sneaky and slippery as an African coral snake.
Even if it's cracking easy to break,
It gives a place to hide from the mistakes
To let your heart overtake,
Let your love awake,
And play an ominous game
To claim the untame,
And find what appears to be almost fake
When you're with your past sits with you by a drained lake,
And your crush loves you and your mind pushes out the word ache,
Makes it irresistible to forget the world awake,
So you can live in the perfect place, a kingdom without mistakes.

As I Sit
by Tyler Eller

As I sit and wonder
I begin to ponder
Staring off into far yonder.
Thinking about why life is tough
And how the going's getting rough.
Having to shut out all this stuff.
Because of school and parents
Everything becomes stressful.
Her arms are my only safe haven
Where I can experience something blissful.

Inspired By the Unknown
by Emily Reiter

Space is so large
And yet, still growing.
That vast emptiness
Is simply breathtaking.
The stars glimmer
With untamed beauty.
Planets, still undiscovered,
Spark our imagination.
Nebulas, black holes, and quasars
Continue to inspire us.
A place where the known and unknown collide,
Shattering across our universe.
With all its complexity,
The beauty of space still manages to captivate us.

Ode To the Coffin
by Hannah Demerchant

Just five minutes
It will be the perfect amount of time
Five toasty minutes
I put on my alien-like goggles to protect my corneas at all costs
Lotion soaks into my skin like a sponge in dirty dishwater
The lid closes and my days of life get slimmer
The ultraviolet lights burn my skin like macaroni when you forget the water
Anything to not resemble a Twilight character
Five minutes turns into a power nap
The warmth wraps around me like a tortilla wrapped around meat and cheese
The light clicks off and cools my sweaty body
as if I'm a flea being blown off a dog
Just a few minutes in a coffin - How can it hurt anyone?
Before I know it, my next five minute death appointment is scheduled

Decide
by Tracy Show

You were a pretty image on the outside
Saying hi and showing everyone your good side
Having everyone on your side
But no one knew what was really inside
No one knew how cruel it was inside
No one knew what you were keeping hidden on the inside
You caused everyone to be against my side
Making them throw me aside
And that's why I decide
To leave your side

Dear Soulmate
by Laura Rivera

From a cold and windy December night
Two small, bright and shining eyes came to life.
Your honey-like smile filled me with delight
And through my mind happiness was rife.
I find joy in the small things that bond us
Like every single petal to its rose.
The differences that complement us are glorious.
We are a match no one else can compose.
We never seem to stray far from each other
Because how could the moon drift away from the stars?
Since I am the sister and you are the brother
Together our light glows brighter than quasars.
What you mean to me I cannot express
Yet I hope you know how much I love you nonetheless.

Maybe
by Faith McGhee

Maybe sunsets fade away to remind us that nothing lasts forever ...
Maybe flowers wilt to remind us
that even the beautiful and seemingly perfect will fade ...
Maybe hearts break to remind us that people can change ...
Maybe memories fade to remind us that we need to leave our past in the past ...
Maybe we grow up to remind ourselves that we can and will get better
and looking back only makes us children once more ...
Maybe people grow distant to remind themselves
that nobody is worth their pain or hurt ...
Maybe people grow silent to remind themselves of what they've lost ...
Maybe people pray to remind themselves that a God is all they have ...
Maybe people go blind to remind themselves
that even the brightest colors can fade ...
Maybe people die to remind themselves that they don't last forever ...

Touch
by Alexis Henry

I crave your soft touch as air I need breath
from dawn till dusk,
a heavy sigh I heave.
Fingertips lightly brushing the surface
Sending a pleasing shiver through me
like a glass of frigid water - refreshing.
You, I need.
Though air need I breathe, your touch I need so.
Much pleasure is given,
My need only grows.
Like a flower in a meadow
The rays of light fall upon,
I lust for a touch from someone for now,
Who is gone.

Hedgehog
by Chaewon Oh

I see the herd of hedgehogs is passing by me
hedgehogs with keen prickles
keep a distance from others
for they could not get from other's prickles
I am also like a hedgehog
sometimes want to get along with people
but feel stifled
On the contrary, if I get farther away from people
I feel solitary
The dilemma of a hedgehog can't separate from our life

Flaming Passion
by Jacob Tanner

Once I saw you, I'd pledged you to be sought.
A fire ignites for thee, prompt to begin.
You had something about you, just so hot!
Kindled passion, consuming all within.
Looking from afar, dying from the heat,
the heat your presence brings: an inferno.
Your presence rendering me obsolete ...
I cannot take it any longer! Oh!
Your aura emitting pure perfection,
filling me with intoxicating lust.
I strive for your company, affection.
To be together ... we have to ... we must!
You are the one, it couldn't be clearer.
Alas, my love ... you're trapped in the mirror.

Peace Amidst Chaos
by David Hoxsie

Indifference strikes hard at my core,
with different thoughts among my mind.
One wreaks my mind store,
another looks more kind.
I open my heart, mind, and body to this being,
it's stronger than I thought.
I find it close to my heart more, and only after leaning,
I learned it exists only after I sought.
It took great pain, grieving, love, and loss,
before I finally found it, it's peace amidst chaos.

What Did I Do?
by Alix Mouradian

What did I do, I do not know
How did I do it, that won't show
Will I do it again, I'll never know
For why did this happen you'll never know
I'm tired of trying
I'm sick of lying
I'm always smiling
But I'm actually crying
It's so difficult to describe
Forgiveness isn't what I want
What I want is to be able to flaunt
Not a smile, that won't happen for a while
You gave up on me
While I gave up on us.

Who Am I?
by Aubrey McGhee

Raised by a mother and knew no father
Heard plenty of stories, but knew no truth
I grew older and felt like a bother
For wanting to know more about my youth
Part of me felt like a gaping hole
One question asked, "Who was I meant to be?"
Finding who I am is my one true goal
My one true goal could simply set me free
Hidden away from a part of myself
Longing to have part of the other half
How do I listen to "just be yourself"
Is a part of me just a photograph?
A whole of two halves, broken apart
Unknown part, only to create a pure heart

Arrival
by Tate Elliott

I pour my entire soul blood and energy
into a life that is only
temporary; saturating
myself into a life
better left unknown.
I simply cannot know
what living a balanced life
feels like.
Willing to clench my feet in their
lap upon instances too strenuous
to stand, but,
Who finds it acceptable to
leave and arrive all at once?

Until We Sink
by Hannah Greiner

Life is a euphemism for treading water until we sink.
An act of living so perpetual we dare not ask nor even question.
It's not until the kicking seizes that our bodies drag us under;
A thrill of tantalizing fear, a landscape of brilliant shades of blue.
The light above us dims as we slip further down;
Descending into silence, swallowed by the sea.
A certain depth, a certain darkness
A feeling of contentment plunged into black.
No more agonies, no more burdens
Just a gratitude of endless bliss.
Forever breathing in the sea.

The Musician In the Forest
by Rachel Tice

It was a warm, clear, summer day in May
When the Musician sat in the green grass
A cold breeze came as he started to play
his strong instrument of exquisite brass
Nearby birds heard this and began to sing
rabbits started thumping their feet in beat
the squirrels and chipmunks began to swing
and all these creatures gathered at his feet
The Musician started to play louder
as the forest creatures started to dance
the forest burst to life like gunpowder
All the creatures caught in a kind of trance
The Musician slowed as the creatures depart
The Musician takes his music to heart

County Delight
by Nicolas McClure

I'm not very formal
I don't wear suits
I'd rather do ranch work
While wearing my boots,
I'm recognized as young
I love cake topping
And if I had the money I'd go tack shopping
Get the tractor and put out some hay
Try to holster my animals
But they wouldn't stay
Farm work is hard day and night
I believe I lost my herd
I can't see them in sight

Leila
by Layla Kettler

I lie in bed slowly drifting off to sleep
I am soon awakened by my goat going into labor
I jump to my feet and sprint outside
"I do not want to miss this!" I say to myself
I walk into the barn and I see her
On the cold cement, wrapped in blankets that were supposed to keep her warm
But those blankets did nothing
As I was brought back to reality I see my dad trying to save her
But even he couldn't help her
As I look at her cold lifeless body on the floor,
a lonely tear starts to form in my eye
And once I realize this was not a dream that lonely tear fell
And soon after, I left her there – just like she left me.

Wind
by Audrey Kaspar

There isn't much to this bitter chill that caresses even the most bitter faces.
It has seen all; every race so unique and beautiful.
It has seen their emotions and every impulse.
When they become angry with one another,
it brings them together by destroying what they love most.
Some may know it as destructive,
though it pollinates their fields and brings them flowers.
Some find comfort in it when it dries their tears.
Some fear it because it is more powerful than their vainly built towers.
Some know it as an enigma because it is everywhere, though they cannot see.
It is connected with them all, especially when they are divided.
There isn't much to this soft warmth that caresses even the most cold of hearts.

Inflamed
by Cassidy Bauer

She gazed into the sun
With the smokin' thoughts
Of her love
And let herself burn
For him.

Chains
by Makenzie Macy

They wrap around my chest
and dig into my skin
My words stop in my throat
cold fingers wrapped and thin
My heart wreaks havoc
with the questions that I'm asking
I taste of copper and rust
it coats my lungs and leaves me gasping
The metal clinks together
I smell of dirt and blood
I hang from the rafters
And succumb to the flood
I give up on the fight
My vision is blurred and faded
This is my last night
My mind is serrated

2 AM
by Jenna Cornett

Inside my head in the dead of night is the most peaceful place I know
Without a voice, feeling or light to disturb the comfort and warmth
That moment, when all is still, is the most cherished thing that I own
I slug through school and life and stress just so I can return to my real home
That nothingness teaches me more than anything outside of it could
The silence makes me ponder over things I'd never otherwise explore
I study the world, I study myself, I take a class that doesn't exist
And then I smile or laugh or cry and remember that I'm just a human
In the darkness, there's no reason to conceal inherent imperfections
In such a place,
I can throw away the trials of the previous day and the one ahead
Until eventually sleep arrives and puts an end to that night's contemplation
When the morning comes,
I can't stay huddled inside the sheltered nest of my bed
The sun drags me out from the illusion of serenity under my heavy blankets
And once again, another hectic day will steal every trace of repose
But I'll be fine if I hold on to the remains of my own 2 AM

The Winter Weather
by Kourtney Davidson

The air around us is so frigid and cold.
We hustle in and out so fast,
but we all act so bold
in order to last.
The sun hardly shines,
and the snow won't go away.
The kids go out to make designs,
and it's like this every day.
After a long, long wait,
the air finally warms up.
Everyone begins to feel great,
but the mud starts to build up.

Parents
by Trelin Thomas

They are there every morning,
They are there every night,
They teach you the ways to live through your life.
Through lessons, teaching and so much more,
They cover you in shelter from the ceiling to the floor.
Whenever you make a mistake,
They give new ideas that we all take.
Morals, manners and loving compassion,
Taking care of us is an uneasy passion.
While it's not easy I can bet,
They help us out when we're upset.
No matter what they are always caring
No matter what I love my parents!

Losing the Internet
by Christena Matzeder

What would you do if one day the internet just stopped
Would your world come crashing down
I mean it's so great when your computer freezes
Or your email is overloaded with spam
How about seeing all the senseless posts about what someone does of a day
It's so important to get the most likes on each selfie you post
Would you feel less important if you didn't see all of the drama-filled posts
But you just HAVE to believe everything you read on the internet
People would be forced to actually have a conversation with each other
and that's a horrible idea
We can just nonchalantly talk bad about everyone on social media instead
What would you do if one day the internet just stopped
Would we have anything left to our humanity

Paths
by Anna Allen

Path One,
Childhood ignorance
Path Two,
Innocent bliss
Path Three,
Empty deeds
Path Four,
Misguided feelings
Path Five,
Clinging to fear
Path Six
Dreaded crying smear
Path Seven,
Invisible barrier, painful wall
Path Eight,
Almost wearing a marriage shawl
Now on Path Nine,
I promise I won't delay.
No more steering left or right.
I will reach you someday.

Tomboy Confessions
by Mads Rosentreter

"You're in the men's section," they say with their eyes
"I know," I sigh without actually sighing,
lowering my gaze so I can't hear them anymore
Mom used to tell me that
Back when I first started wearing button-ups that weren't fitted
She doesn't tell me anymore, just asks questions
It's not really plural, just the one
"Are you a boy?"
Of course
Sometimes I forget masculine girls are not really girls
We are something new and foreign, something to change and fix
I don't know if my mom thinks I'm fixable or not,
But she must think I am damaged
"I love you to the moon and back," she tells me every night
But she was so broken-hearted she almost cried
when I cut my hair short the first time
Chastised me when I said I didn't want to shave anymore
Told me to save the shoes I hated in case I changed my mind
I have always been the disappointment destined to destroy our family
I know she says she loves me, but when we are shopping for my baby brother
She puts back a car seat for being too girly
I realize that all she wants is a kid who isn't me

Show Cattle
by Tanner Shipman

Every day I wake up in the morning over the summer.
I do the chores to feed the cattle with my papa.
They are mooing for their breakfast like babies
Every day going by fast.
I'm old enough to show cattle.
Then I had a responsibility to wake up every day
of the summer to work with my cattle.
I wash them and brush their fur.
Their fur is soft like silk.
I got help from my papa and my aunt all the time.
Then as time went by
when got a little older to do it on my own.
But when my papa passed away
I had to work harder every day.
Every day I did the chores in the early mornings and late evenings.
Every day I work with my show cows to get them ready for shows.
As my papa passed, I won more rewards at my shows.
I always worked hard to win my shows.
My favorite show year was this year and two years ago.
My favorite show Steer was Eli and my Heifer was Dreamqueen.

Honestly
by Emily Cousino

TBH I'm never completely honest
Never have I truthfully told someone all of the things it takes to be me
To be honest my true self isn't the person you meet in the halls
or the person you encounter when I speak up in class.
I spare people my honesty because honestly
I fear being interjected by rejection.
I question all the knowledge I lend all the connections I begin.
When I'm honest my honesty gets me honestly
a hard pill swallowed leaving me all hallowed
so TBH I wear a mask, I craft it with the paintbrush of my mind
so you don't have to see what's inside
I have a mask for every occasion
giving my mind a Freudian mistake of conscious confetti cake.
Layered with too much conscious mind making my id hide deep, deep inside
TBH ... I'm not honest.
But honestly I want to be.
I want you to know me
yes I wear masks and am not honestly the real me
but the only way for me to de-layer the cake in my brain
and forsake the way I've been trained.
Is to show you Emily Anne Cousino,
show you honestly my honest me. Show you the mind I hide inside.

The Bush
by Rachel Harding

In a field unknown to humankind, there is a bush in many colors.
To us it might seem very rare, but to them it is contrare.
They flaunt it with the best of colors, while we just stare at its many wonders.
So for us to see something so neat, we have to be something like a tree.
So always remember to keep your eyes, so that in the future there are no lies.

Will You Take the Opportunity?
by Olivia Felicelli

Will you take the opportunity,
To become something greater?
See through the pity,
Find the laughter.
To become something greater,
It is no ordinary task.
Find the laughter,
Look behind people's fake masks.
It is no ordinary task,
To become the best.
Look behind people's fake masks.
You are blessed,
To become the best.
So, see through the pity,
And achieve that dream of yours.
Will you take the opportunity?

Four Seasons
by Christopher Atwood

The four seasons filled with delight.
Left with the coldest at night.
Fall, when you lose the ones you love.
Winter, drowning the world in ice.
Spring, a day to recline the Earth.
Summer, a day to break from your chains.
The four seasons filled with delight.
When spring cleanses the Earth tonight.
Summer, summer break free from your chains tonight.
Fall, fall mourn the ones you lost tonight.
Fall ends, and winter begins to destroy the bad and bring in the new.
Four seasons filled with delight.
Spring is the best way to life.
Four ways this world is cleansed from the evil on this land.
The four seasons filled with delight.
Left with the coldest at night.

A Dream
by Shailyn Ross

A pile of hope mingles in my mind,
the dissonance tugging at my heartstrings;
ribcage concert halls fill with the sound
of marcato memories in the making.
And dancing to the decibels of my dreams,
crescendoing in sync is a symphony
of pianissimo possibilities yet to be composed.

Tired Trees
by Griffon Rice

Trees are tired
They breathe all day
Willows and pines
Standing and waiting
For a new day
A new adventure
But they just wait
The trees are so tired
The willows weep
The pines cry a sticky sap
Sticky, tired tears
The trees are tired
The more tired they get
The more they want to run
But the trees are too tired to run

Blank
by Veronica Blissick

Blank page—no words, no voice.
Blinking cursor—a loss of hope.
Our lives seem to have no meaning, no point
When blank
A canvas without paint
The can of color unopened
A blindfold over their eyes.
And then you take it off—you take it off your own eyes.
A wordless page and a paintless canvas
Only mean you have to give it your own meaning
Your own purpose
The blank page and empty canvas are no longer
The demons that controlled you
You have the key to the locked door—
By opening your eyes.

Gator
by Olivia Simma

It was a Thursday in late September.
How could I not remember?
The day you left to gallop high in the sky.
Our unbreakable bond will forever be tied.
Your hoofprint will always be on my heart.
I knew I loved and cherished you from the start.
7 unforgettable years with you by my side.
You found and gave me everything I thought I needed to hide.
Unconditional love for my Heart Horse.

The Wraith
by Dallas Fennell

Cometh death thou hasn't perfect haste,
You stole our hearts to decline our faith.
Touching our souls filling us with hate,
You're not demon nor monster but a wraith.
Give us grief with silence and make us more,
Using heartfelt love in swollen prayers.
But please never take what we had before,
Instead for our vows please give us theirs.
All broken spirits cry for all of their wrongs.
While most souls improve while they can.
When the dreaded play and sing the old wraith song,
Comes the ashes of grief birthing all of man.
All alive or dead will come as it stands,
That man shall not rise but by God's hands.

Foster Puppy Love
by Isabella Dolot

You came to me just shy of nine weeks old
Very small and black and oh so furry
Four big wet paws, your jet black nose so cold
I wondered if you'd love me, no worry
Those brown eyes remind me of baby deer
Your tail wags quickly, thump, thump, wallop, swoosh
Puppy teeth sharp like needles, new ones near
First the puddle, water, grass, mud, then smoosh
You are quickly growing right before me
Time for a new leash and a red collar
Let's go for a walk past this pretty tree
Run, then come, when I give you a holler
Foster dog, tears come like water then fall
Only one more month till turn-in, wish you were still small

Dracula
by Luke Chappa

In the dark he lurks
His perks are above all other
He rules viciously
And maliciously
For he controls the dark
Be careful in the park
His army is ruthless
And you will be clueless
For when he comes
You will hear his drums
This lord of darkness
They call ... Dracula!

D-Day Upon Us
by William McVey

We storm the beach in hope of victory.
But we only fall short on defeat.
Underestimating our enemies we charge
We move like a furious storm
Only to meet the ends of their barrels.
The Axis have prepared for this moment.
They only wait for our arrival.
The battlefield like walking through the gates of Hell
As we try to make our way to Heaven.
We wait for a sign, a miracle to signal victory.
Then finally we see it.
And then we see it, God giving us a sign.

What's Left Behind
by Stephanie Fowler

A quiet structure stands tall.
Poles with chipped blue paint reveal splotches of red and orange.
The structure is surrounded by slides, ladders, and stairs,
Abandoned after years of use.
Poles with chipped blue paint reveal splotches of red and orange.
What was once filled with screaming children is now quiet,
abandoned after years of use.
but nothing else.
What was once filled with screaming children is now quiet.
The structure is surrounded by slides, ladders, and stairs,
but nothing else.
A quiet structure stands tall.

The Gray Areas
by Katelyn So

In screaming color, I am grayscale
In valiant flavor, I am plain; stale
The world moves fast
I stay in place
I am as blank as the look on my face
The feeling isn't ice
Or fire, it's stone
It's nothing, it's bland
But it's much like quicksand
I sink in it, standing
I can't do much more when it tugs at my core
The truth is depression is more than just sad
It's regret, anger, hatred
When nothing's that bad
Nothing's quite right, and you don't quite belong
But you can't bring it to light
So you just move along
Because time keeps on moving
Life still goes on
You'll just never know just what is wrong

For the Soul To Reach Success
by Caleb Stone

Dreams which feel like reality,
For the hopeful eyes, there's a future to see.
Thought to be a mirage, unbeknownst to what one can achieve.
Slowly discovering these capabilities.
What seems to be a ludicrous passion,
Is a world only dreamers imagine.
To the blind, it is something one cannot fathom;
But to those with a vision, these dreams can happen.
As an ending scene leaves one filled with emotion,
These wishes begin a path to endless devotion.
Though young minds may seem filled with delusion,
There's beauty and bravery in being so free-spoken.
This urge of a desire to chase,
Will lead this child to a successful place.
Please-- allow these goals to be embraced;
For it is the only way to find motivation in their days.
Dedication and zest
Is your child's sole life vest.
To stay afloat, do not make their dreams feel oppressed--
Instead, stay by their side, fondly aiding them as they progress.

Broken
by Samuel Allar

Feeling in the dark
Never ready to embark
In no way a spark
I wish I could just disembark
Disembark and de-mark
All this hurt
Just in the dirt
In all ways to revert
Revert back
Back to the old ways
The bad days
The unacceptable ways
Damaged and broken
That's all I am
Like a garbage can
Just one small man
That's all I am
But I am strong
I can prolong
Prolong the ways

The Ant
by Kayla Birsching

Everyone's expectations of what I should be,
The weight of the world on my shoulders I hold,
I feel like all eyes are always on me,
I'm like an ant magnified under a microscope,
The heavy weight of society's,
Expectations and standards grow,
The pile just gets bigger and crushes me,
I'm only a tiny ant, you know!
They watch closely through the lens just to catch my mistakes,
Just so that they can point them out,
Onto me they project their angst and self-hate,
And criticism they bring about,
Most who peer through the microscope's lens,
Watch for a while, then go away,
The people file out, the women and men,
But one person always remains,
I wonder who's always there to criticize,
I finally look up and see,
But the person I see is the biggest surprise,
My own worst critic is me.

The Forest Mother
by McKenna Podolak

In the heart of a timeless forest,
Lies a garden prepared by a devilish florist,
Hellebore flowers border a deceased tree,
Silently awaiting for the apogee.
The fateful day the twin brother birds rise,
Is the day the world will meet her demise,
As they pluck their feathers,
And conjoin together,
They become the sapling from the nether.
The sprout thrives on evil intent,
On pain and suffering and fatal torment,
Its trunk grows stronger from the people's throes,
As destruction comes swiftly to the meadows,
Its roots burrow deep into the earth,
As it awaits her grand rebirth.
The Forest Mother,
Trapped in an eternal state of pother,
With the antlers of a deer,
And an aura of drear,
Her being is one who time itself reveres.

The Old Pendulum Clock
by Dan Hardy

Forever standing tall in its oaken case
Singing Westminster, with three weights, and a face.
Some people to a drummer of their own walk
As for me I march to a grandfather clock,
Just the tick tock of a pendulum clock.
A gift from an old man to his lady wife.
That timepiece would come to shape family life.
Ever present. All knowing. "Y'all stay in time."
Its presence shown by the quarterly song's chime.
There for all to see, our sentinel sublime.
Marking off the minutes to keep all in stride,
Ever true, pendulum swinging side to side.
Passed down through the generations, hall to hall.
Ever guiding those who heed its hourly call.
Tick, tock - a gentle reminder for us all.
In life, far and wide I hope to range and roam,
Never losing my way, over grass and loam.
It'll just take one lil' sound to call me home,
If I'm the next one lucky enough to stock
The tick tock of that old pendulum clock.

Memory
by Isabelle Light

Memories from the past
Kept in a book so they'll last
I look through the pictures
My mind flashes back
A fun family visit
Short, yet sweet
Every activity great
And yummy things to eat
I recall the competitiveness when playing games
Winning was a mission
My favorite part, meeting a family addition
So cute and so small
I remember the happiness in my heart
The feeling now dull
When it was time to go home, I wanted to stay
Tried to hold back the tears
Saying goodbye was the hardest
I had to remind myself I'd be back the next year
My heart aches to go back to the past
For those were the good days and life goes by too fast

Ode To the Love of Art
by Jared McCormick

With the simple stroke from the brush in hand,
Focusing on the beauty of motion,
Adding color to land that once was bland,
Soft and smooth the paint spreads just like lotion.
Although a skill seemingly lost in time,
When art was seen as a passage to Heaven–
And not just a piece to a rich man's eye–
Gave artists their form of a confession,
With the simple stroke from the brush in hand.
A mixture of sweet sweat and tasteful blood,
And a brush to smooth the anomalies,
A working hand will bring upon a flood,
To which the judgmental eye shall be pleased.
Truly never a mistake in this Piece,
Every stroke has its part in the Account.
Telling stories to put the mind to peace,
The hours spent– not knowing the amount.
Oh how masterpieces seem to fade 'way,
Comes the hope of revival modern day,
With the simple stroke from the brush in hand.

The Human Race, Are We
by Gabriella Smith

A world anew
That is all I for one wish for
For even in the depths of darkness I can feel the embrace of morning's light
Far too gone in the earth's negative grasp
Means only a delay
As I am to realize just like all others
I am the hero that I have always wished for
That we all have in us
Our own light to shine
Given what little we are
We can make big adjustments from more than enough scraps of the past
The future is to faithfully unveil the unknown reaching everything
It's all we as people could ever want or need
It is all we ever obsess over
Time is just an obstacle we overcome upon the way
Beautifully and gracefully exhibiting every face of our flaws
Humans are only human
That of which is a simple saying
Simple and yet speaking in volumes
Is the human race, are we

Blind
by Thomas Norman

I walk these burning streets, my pained heart full of shame
Knowing that I did not want this, but yet I'm left to blame
People dying or being tortured is all I have in sight
My young age has left expanding to this painful plight.
Selling my soul with every move I tend to make
Dreaming dreams before I begin to wake
Every dream is far but grateful
But much worse is that they may be fateful
My bad choices have led to a curse
Only my feelings left to be reimbursed
People trying to kill me everywhere that I go
I still remember that young boy from a little bit ago
Who thought the world was sunshine and full of rainbows
He saw happiness when he looked out the windows
He saw red flowers sprouting from the faithful ground
Not blood stains from the people struck down
He saw cool bubbles floating in the ocean water
Not the person fighting, sinking underwater
This young boy was great, but couldn't see
Now I do though, because this young boy was me

Pen and Paper
by Clara Scott

With this pen, Lord may you write
of the things not yet in sight
my future plans
are in your hands
may your will over my life
be fulfilled without strife
With this paper, light as a feather
your hands shall keep it from torturous weather
Lord, if I may or if I might
lead me towards another night
so that I may glorify you
in everything that I do
With my will on pen and paper
my life is only just a vapor
Lord, may my life praise your name
not for me and my future fame
but for You, the creator
of all things seen in this life
Lord, you are my provider
and may I praise you day and night

The Dunes
by Allison Dill

I'm going to swallow the sand
To become the dunes that you've made me
I'm going to accept your hate
And I'm going to let it destroy my body
I'm going to wear my heart in a locket
So I may remember my soul before you wrecked me
I need the sand to trickle through my lungs
So they may know the hate you filled me with
Can you feel me now?
Now that you've drowned me in this desert ...
Can you hear me now?
Now that you've killed me ...
I'm a brash example of devotion
I'm a fool for fortitude
I'm barren,
And embarrassing
You've stripped me down
To just sand and fear
But I've built myself a shelter
And I'm living with it now

Rise
by Tyler Schmalzried

Look to the sky
Can't you see that everything is brighter?
The hues of morning have come,
Banishing the darkness that seeped into your dreams
Look around you
The birds are singing again
Their sounding melodies distract from any worries,
And their brilliant affirmations make old harsh words seem insignificant
Look down at yourself
You have been kicked and broken
Left with nothing and expected to give everything
But listen to me
Yesterday has come and gone, and with it all its trials and tribulations
All that is left is you
You must pick yourself up off the cold, hard ground
And declare that nothing can break you without your permission
Overcome your fears
Overcome your hesitation
The sun has risen
It's time for you to rise with it

A Dream Deferred Is a Dream Worth Fighting For
by Rebeka Cooper

A dream worth living is a dream worth working for,
Through blood, sweat, and tears striving for more,
Dreams deferred left as whispers in the wind,
Do not seem to know the beginning from the end.
Dreams are like caterpillars on a twig,
They eventually grow wings colorful and big,
They transform into butterflies, these caterpillars do,
They go through battles, battles of life they must push through.
The butterfly tries harder and harder striving to win,
Pushing through heart-pounding trials, through thick and through thin,
Through many failures at life it may seem,
The butterfly perched on that lonely twig thinks about its shattered dream.
The butterfly takes off again, heart full of pride,
It takes off to the sky with its wings spread wide,
The butterfly reaches the end of the valley, and journey that seemed,
Too hard to accomplish and push through that shattered dream.
Only you can accomplish and push through these tough times,
These times of hardship like that hard-working butterfly,
Never give up if your dream seems to defer,
For in the end, you will accomplish what you have been striving for.

Too Close
by Lillian Caister

It was never intended to be
For us to be together
It was a crime for me
To take you from them.
It was for my entire life
That you stayed by my side
It was total bliss for me
To keep you from them.
It's every night after nine
You chase the monsters away
It's a wonderful dream for me
To hide you from them.
It's now too late
For you to stay any longer
It's growing too old for me
To stay from them.
It will never be the same
For you to be away
It will be a nightmare for me
To be without you.

Reminiscent
by Madison Corriveau

As I look down at your picture, it's like I've fallen asleep
I see myself in that room again, watching you as I weep
Your outstretched hand holding mine, your heart beating slow
I desperately held on tighter, refusing to let you go
As you took your final breath, I saw you look at me
And I knew that your last moments here were beautiful and free
A caring, charming presence that was taken way too soon
Everyone could sense the moment when your soul had left the room
A sparkle had diminished, a fire without a flame
We said goodbye one by one while God called you home by name
But now, years later, we look back and relish in what we had
A grandfather, a brother, a husband, and a dad
Our lives have changed without you, but in a sense are still the same
For we can see you in our world each and every day
A random act of kindness from a stranger on the street
Or the way we sense your strength when we have fallen to our knees
You fought for us every day though you knew you'd lose
You played a game you couldn't beat and accepted that as truth
As cancer stole your final minutes, I prayed for just one more
You may have lost the battle, Papa, but to us you won the war

(Un)Broken
by Gabrielle Udell

They say it's broken, but don't know why.
Can we fix it? A sweet, naive child asks unknowingly.
No response is uttered as there isn't a manual to follow, or rules to go by.
They call the plumber to try and stop the incessant leaks,
but he cannot stop them.
They call the exterminator to get rid of all the pests,
but he cannot get rid of them.
What do we do? The same naive child asks. Nothing.
There is nothing we can do but wait.
Wait to see if it can heal alone, but it's unlikely.
Days, weeks, years seem to go by. The naive child turns into a young man,
But it is still broken and he still asks, what do we do?
To this day the answer remains the same. Nothing.
There is nothing we can do but wait.
Wait to see if it can heal alone, but it's still unlikely.
So they wait. And do nothing.
They do nothing, and nothing changes.
She will remain broken, damaged, and dormant.
Until someone can finally fix her,
But the question is who?

Morning Rush
by Maddisen Chinavare

The mornings with my family are never a bore
I'm super happy because I'm hot mess number four.
We have a turtle sloth who looks for his "contacts,"
And a dad who sometimes overreacts.
And a mom who works her butt off,
To get everything set and ready for the day,
Without her, our minds would be so far away.
She gets us rip-roaring, and ready to go,
But without all of us, there would be no show.
We are a team, my family and I,
Our "team" is like a table, it has four people to hold up each side.
When one of us is hot mess number one
The rest become happy because they have not won
The title of being the blobfish,
Which is something we all don't wish.
I love my family through and through
And while one may be slow and the other be feisty,
Mornings are only a little bit dicey.
We are a team, my family and I,
We are strong, and we know how to fly.

Rules
by Sarah Zeller

Pills and hideaways have always been there.
Friends can't come over, that's because we care.
Couches and bedrooms are good for hiding.
Even the swings will work; pretend you're flying.
Ignore the shouts that the neighbors can hear.
Don't spill the overflowing bags of cans labeled 'beer'.
Don't come out of your room or go back inside.
No use in talking; their brains are fried.
Don't ever dare to ask to spend time together.
That's the phone's job; like the boy for the weather.
Tread lightly for every step you dare to take,
When anger comes, courage you must fake.
You may not cry, fidget, speak, or look away,
Look directly into the eyes and still you must stay.
The moment a single tear falls to the ground
Is the moment when everything comes crumbling down.
Stop your crying, it is what makes it worse.
Their anger will build up and fester like a curse.
It's your fault this happened, it always will be.
This is why you can't ever stop saying 'sorry'.

Dreams
by Shianne Howard

10:00 pm with happy dreams of beautiful scenery,
Unicorns, with chocolate bark trees
With cotton candy as leaves, candy bees
And cute fluffy animals
But it doesn't always stay that way ...
When candy bees turn into killer bees.
When darkness sets over the scenery,
Cotton candy starts to melt,
The chocolate bark
Turns into poison apple
The once beautiful scenery is now black
Cute fluffy animals turn into skeletons
And now it's a nightmare.
The type that brings fear into the air,
Where you feel as if it's real,
You try to pinch your arm to wake up.
It doesn't work. You see a demon in your head run towards you
Then you wake up from what feels like hours
You look at the clock, 10:05 pm, how did the time go by so slow
When you have that question ask the demon in your dreams.

Thank You
by Kyle Bragg

I hate you, but not as much as I hate myself.
I hate that you left me, to fend for myself.
I hate you, because I love you.
I hate the pain you put me through.
I must say thank you, through all the anger and tears.
I must say thank you because I want to be the better version of you.
I don't want to be the person consumed by liquid evils like you.
I don't want to end up like you.
I won't turn out like you.
I will just say thank you.
All I can say is thank you,
Thank you for hurting me because you made my weaknesses my strengths.
Thank you for making me stronger.
Thank you for making me see the evils
that lurk in the shadows of broad daylight.
The evils that fill us with disorientation of life,
if we are not careful or cautious of our actions.
Thank you.
I love you.
Thank you Dad, I really do love you.

A Dusty, Old Book
by Olivia Blissick

"A few minutes is all it will take," he replied as if stating fact.
He lays out the worksheet on my desk.
The first question is full of infinite depth:
Did Gatsby truly love her like he said?
Instantly, every moment Gatsby and Daisy had is in my head.
He waited for her, gave everything to her,
But—
I am suddenly haunted by the memory of my first love.
Like Gatsby, he gave me so much,
Although, for every gift, he wanted
And the minute I refused,
We were done.
Is that love?
"Time's up!" He declares.
I whip my head around,
All pencils are down.
The term "shock" barely captures the essence of the state I'm in.
No uproar for this great injustice?!
The time given was nowhere near enough.
But to them, it's just another dusty, old book.

IDK What I'm Doing
by Devin Otrompke

IDK what I'm doing
How do you write a poem?
I just don't understand.
Do you just print some words?
Hope they have meaning?
Or do you think real hard,
To have an effect?
Is it the choice of words, or the message?
Do you write about love, or an inside depression?
I don't know how to write poems,
Maybe if I add a little rhyme—
I feel free only when I fly
In the peaceful blue sky.
Do I say stuff that just has a deeper meaning—
So restricted from reality, is it meant for me
To fight within my head for a grasp of it?
Are poems just for love, and kindness—
Looking into the depths of your eyes ocean blue eyes
I can see my future in you.
How do you write a poem?
I just don't understand

Bodies
by Laura Hicken

Hands.
They point me towards different directions.
Pull me this way and that.
Push me to and from their ideas of a good future.
Striking down my wants, dreams, and ideas.
Eyes.
Scrutinize my dreams, seeking out every possible flaw.
They roll to show disapproval
Cry to find my sympathy and silent submission
And close to show disappointment.
Mouths.
They bark directions at me.
Insults and cutting words
Hide beneath the blanket of "kind suggestions" and constructive criticism.
They press in a thin line to show disappointment and rage
stirring beneath the surface.
Noses are turned upwards to show power.
Heads are turned away from the damage they are creating.
Bodies.
Bodies all around me are determining and shaping my future
into what they want.
I can't even remember what I want anymore.

Love vs. Hate
by Grant Watson

Love
Happy, beautiful
Caring, comforting, blessing
Heart, warmth, black, cold
antagonizing, objecting, disgusting
Cold-hearted, ugly
Hatred

I Hope
by Jody Zimmerman

I hope you step on a Lego
I hope your shoelaces come undone
I hope you always burn your Eggo
And that you constantly drive into the sun
I hope you forget your keys in your car
I hope that it rains on your mail
I hope you get locked out of the bathroom
After drinking four pints of ale
I hope that your hair is always caught in your chair
And that you stub your pinky toe, too
I hope that, at some point, you're chased by a bear
And your paint is never the right hue
I hope that it's the small things that make you mad
But in the end, I hope you're glad

Dragon Ascent
by Nathaniel Burke

From the ground they could be seen as they soar
Oh if this could grow to come and be one
Spread these large wings and give a mighty roar
A silhouette under the mighty sun
It stretches and sparks a brilliant flame
Listens to the wars' booming, dooming drum
So it could then chance a glorious claim
And hark thy mark after a kingdom come
Though small it can now prey on those above
Retribution all the previous pain
This is naught a humble fluttering dove
This is a dragon declaring its reign
The challenge and the battle for power
Calling this to soar higher and higher

Love Is Like a Rose
by Ethan Ensminger

Love is like a rose
Once it blooms it's beautiful and harmless
But then it starts growing along with thorns and pain
Then you've just got to
Let it go
Leaving it behind
And forgetting what hurt you

A Girl's Struggle
by Kalia Hudson

The struggle of some girls.
She's a model and a former winner of a beauty pageant.
She struts with absolute excellence across the stage.
Dreaming to be everyone's favorite, to be wanted, to be loved.
Every day she puts on a smile that radiates like the sun,
her eyes are darling, looking like stars.
Her young makeup is flawless, demonstrating her artistic abilities.
Beautiful is what she wants to be and feels worthy of becoming.
But, she has a secret that no one knows.
Behind those sweet daring eyes is a sad girl with low self-esteem.
She doesn't know her worth, what makes her unique, or what she wants in life.
Peer pressure makes her feel as though she can't be herself.
She soon realized to know that she is deserving
of anything harmless or beneficial that comes her way.

Nothing Like the Stars
by Alexis Carlson

A pit bull's eyes are nothing like the stars
Hazed and gray awaiting to see the light of day
Chained and shackled, a soul stuck behind bars
Waiting patiently, hoping to be whisked away
Coat once glossy and pure, now shows signs of war
Waking every day wondering why it has to be this way
Life reduced to nothing but some big score
Wishing all the pain would just go astray
The medication takes the pain away
A crowd cheering as the lights fade
New scars tell the story of a beaten stray
Sirens blare as the police start to raid
Stars shining bring hope of a new day
But we all know it won't end that way

Run
by Abryanna Waters

My life is a race
I run from everything that controls me, overtakes me, consumes me
But they drag me down—down to the depths
Under the threatening, menacing, drowning waters of life
There is no escape, I say to myself
Everything is pulling me down
The weight of this world, like a thousand tons of steel
Grasping and gripping, unrelenting
Fear consumes me
My head spinning like a tornado
A twister of mistakes, sadness and pain
Waiting to take their hold of me
But a voice—barely audible
Calls out to my aching heart
Get up, it whispers
This is not over yet, you are not done
Run from your pain and heartbreak
The race is not finished, you've only just begun
Run.

The Black of Night
by Marshall Humphrey

In the black sky and quiet of the night
Creatures move about, moving towards their fate.
The silent madness makes everything feel alright
The only way to see is by the moonlight
I need to go home, it's getting late
In the black sky and quiet of the night
The path I am on is long and not bright
As I wander and wander I lose my hate
The silent madness makes everything feel alright
There's a rustle in the weeds, do I need to fight?
No, it was only a rabbit that scared me straight
In the black sky and quiet of the night
I see a mountain at the highest height
Looking up, I think about what awaits
The silent madness makes everything feel alright
I see my home and I'm filled with delight
However I wish could stay out past eight
In the black sky and quiet of the night
The silent madness makes everything feel alright

I Have Dreamed
by Aleigha Sutton

For I have dreamed things you wouldn't believe
My mind learns to fly all through the night
I dream to do things most can't achieve
Sometimes my dreams give me moments to grieve
They remind me of moments when things were alright
For I have dreamed things you wouldn't believe
My dreams give me hope to overachieve
My hopes are big and all very bright
I dream to do things most can't achieve
My dreams allow my thoughts to open and unweave
I have dreams of places full of sun and light
For I have dreamed things you wouldn't believe
I dream to do things most couldn't perceive
My thoughts walk out front and into the spotlight
I do dream to do things most can't achieve
Most people assume that I'd be naive
But people think everything is so black and white
For I have dreamed things you wouldn't believe
I dream to do things most can't achieve

God Said No
by Freddiemae Thompson

Like the wind, like the sun
Like the birds, and like the trees
God's love, grace, and beauty shines upon me
In the midst of beauty, a blossoming flower
There lies always a still but sudden antagonist lying near
The storm, with its roaring waves, and stunning lightning
Purses to strike me, drown me, but however
God said no
The earthquake which shakes beneath my struggles of life
Cracks and crumbles before my very eyes, yes
To my benefit, a hero, a champion, a king
Forced closed the heavy rocks of agony breaking right from underneath
When the enemy wanted my soul to fall in the rocky pit
of doubt, bitterness, and defeat
God said no
Rushing waters of the treacherous flood, truly to press anger, envy,
and hatred upon my spirit
After all rain, wind, and storms
God still said no

A Blue Bird of Song Cry
by Angel Walker

Where's the song without a cry
Where's a cry without a song
I say fly little bird, fly
Be free
Not caged
Be strong
But bold
Why is the bird hurt, but also in pain
If it's only trying to be itself
If it's only trying to live life
Find heart
Find happiness
Be like others
But it only can be itself
I guess it stands out
I guess it's different
Where's a cry without a song
Why is the bird hiding its face, but it sings
I guess the bird is finally heard

A Beautiful Day
by Emily Haeck

The rain outside needs to go away
Having sunshine would bring much delight
I wish for good weather every day
Why does it have to be so gloomy out today
I wanted to go have fun tonight
The rain outside needs to go away
My favorite month of the year is May
The flowers that bloom bring a great sight
I wish for good weather every day
Sitting at home makes me feel like I'm going to decay
I want to go outside and fly a kite
The rain outside needs to go away
I'm forced to stay in bed and lay
Having many days like this brings me fright
I wish for good weather every day
I would never put this moment on replay
Mother Nature will eventually get it right
The rain outside needs to go away
I wish for good weather every day

Motionless
by Kelsey Gibbons

Large glassy eyes, beautiful irises.
Long eyelashes framing innocent eyes.
Pink lips slightly agape,
Detailed faces without flaw.
Soft hair resting on charming faces
Skin white as porcelain, delicate as china.
Small hands in laps and by sides
Perching on shelves, situated on chairs
Motionless—
Glassy eyes brimming with malice
Eyelashes covering eyes, hiding true intentions
Lips whisper underlying schemes
Detailed faces, too perfect, too real
Long hair too human for a doll
Porcelain skin a sickly, translucent white
Hands behind back, hiding, sneaking
Watching from shelves, wickedly waiting
Motionless—
Devious.

Take Me Back
by Rachel Smith

The blue sky and white clouds used to smile back at me.
In my backyard, I played on the swings and sang.
I thought about who I would be in high school.
Children have little worries.
I watched the rain pour, and the snow fall.
The sun shine and the stars glow.
Closing my eyes to listen to the songs of the bugs and birds.
Ten years passed.
Adults have big worries.
My stress, tiredness, and sadness
at one time was calm, awake, and happiness.
I remember waking up to a room full of light.
I remember running up and down grassy hills.
I remember counting how many years I had until graduation on my fingers.
Now, I ran out of years to count.
The journey to the rest of my life starts here.
Take me back.
Back to that little girl sitting on a rock by the stream,
counting away.

Alzheimer's
by Olivia Wingate

You have never failed to make me laugh or smile,
To bring me from my worst to my best.
But you have never failed to make me cry.
But it's not your fault,
It's the horrible creature
Bringing darkness inside you that is to blame.
I have no control over it, you have no control over it,
No one has control over it.
We can't stop it.
I pray for it to be better,
But I can't pray for it to be over.
Some days are better,
Some days are worse.
You are still there,
Somewhere deep down inside.
Even when you don't recognize me,
Even when you aren't you,
I know you love me,
And I will always love you.

School
by Haylee Chubb

School
A place of bad communication.
Where one on one
Is not a thing.
And the class moves too fast for my comprehension.
The smart outweigh the slow,
And do not see the light of 'em.
The slow are the good people.
The ones that pay attention to small details
The ones that have greater appreciation for things
The ones who stop others when they look down
and help them up.
The slow are the real smart.
They contain a power the fake smarts don't.
They know how to live in the real world.
The fake smarts know everything except
For how to live.
The slow pick up on more important things-
School is not one of them.

A Broken Home
by Grace Jacobusse

A home. Filled with laughter,
Filled with love.
A home is a family.
Two parents and many kids.
The kids, they grow up,
They move away.
Just one kid is left to stay,
The laughter had turned to screams,
The love turned into separate beds,
One kid left
One kid hears all,
One kid sees all,
One kid, stuck in the middle of two people.
People who used to love each other,
But now can't stand each other.
That loving home
Became a burning house.
That burning house kept burning,
Until there was nothing left.

Under the Same Moon
by Olivia Siman

Pain.
Tears bleed out of her lifeless beautiful eyes
Sour and bitter words dance in her head
She drowns in sorrow—
alone
A pitch-black sky covers her with a sheet of darkness.
Except there is a faded light
Peering through the dark,
Easing the pain
Blocking any shame
The moon.
The moon who knows all—
The moon who sees all—
Sees and knows she's not—
alone
Tears dry away from her bright beautiful eyes
Sweet and lovely words dance into her head
She rises to rejoice—
Serene.

Love
by Maryam Yousif

Love.
What do you think of love?
What words ripple through your head?
Do any words ripple?
Do you know what love is?
Where did love go?
Did it melt down and dissolve in the grass?
You need love as plants need both water and sun in order to produce.
Love is present when you believe in the person that gives it.
A heart symbolizes love.
The kind of love that indicates the sacrifice, patience, humility, mercy,
strength, and courage of the One.
But if His Mother did not respond courageously with, "Yes"
to the out of the world words, that love would not exist.
His life, death, and resurrection has purchased us the rewards of eternal life.
Your heart will fathom all of that,
when you give it to the One who made it.
Your heart will know what love is, when it is satisfied by our Savior, Jesus Christ
because He is love.

Anxiety Attack
by Amanda Sutton

I could barely breathe as my throat was closing in tight
I needed help, but there was no solution in sight
My fears gripped me in terror and filled my head
Everything was so overwhelming, I wished I was dead
People tried to stop it, but they didn't know what to do
My perception of reality was all askew
They told me to breathe but I was
Everything was foggy, my brain was filled with fuzz
It hurt as all of my muscles were squeezing
Though they tried, this just wasn't easing
It's not their fault, they didn't understand
What else could they do but hold my hand?
Cradled in their arms, I loved them so
Terrified of being alone, I didn't want them to go
My thoughts raced around my head in a flurry
Hopelessness enveloped me as I couldn't help but worry
"When will they leave, how long will this last?"
But I was so busy worrying about the future that the present passed

Sincerely
by Carlos Escobar Quezada

It was sunny day
It was a perfect day to walk in the park
Or to make any dream come true
The perfect day to live in the city of Granacio.
Nothing could ruin this day.
When I saw her, she was the most beautiful!!!!
The most angelic.
The most charming, classy, comely, cute,
dazzling, delicate, delightful, divine,
elegant, enthralling, enticing, excellent, exquisite,
fair, fascinating, fetching, fine, foxy,
good-looking, gorgeous, graceful.
She was the perfect match for me
I could not ask for more
I was not sure if I was going to able to handle it
I just knew that I want her for me
Sincerely, the chair in the yard sale
To the table across the street.

The Brick Wall
by Lance Denham

When I moved to the lake, there was an insurmountable wall in front of me.
it frightened me. When I touched it, it was frozen and icy.
I was stuck there for a while.
Trying to pass through the seemingly, impassable barrier.
Only by learning to hold on to the wall, and caring for it.
Was I able to pass.
The frozen brick wall slowly thawed out.
I took it down piece by piece
I made myself a small quaint little house.
I placed two doors on it, on opposite sides
The first door, a glass door before the brick wall.
So I could always look back at it and remember.
And the other, that door that's missing pieces
On the opposite side of the wall.
I'll be honest that was a design flaw.
Even with a hole in my house. I never touched that last brick, of my wall.
I leave it there sitting in my house,
As a monument for the visitors.

Don't Shoot!
by Sonteé Dumas

Click! Click!
Bang! Bang!
The sound a gun makes when being triggered and fired
Stop where you are and don't move!
Feet apart and put your hands up!
Two officers would say
You stand there and glare, petrified you stare
You want to move but you wouldn't dare
If you move and they shoot you, they wouldn't care
You try to explain but instead of listening, they tell you to shut up
Dealing with the cops, you're just fed up
Hands behind your head and get down on your knees! Now!
Panicking and afraid that they are going to shoot you,
so you just stand there and do nothing
Get down!
The officer jumps on you and now you're on the ground ...
Silence going all around

An Ode To My Cats
by Katie Moore

for all the cats of the world:
fluffy, soft as fair flowers' petals
eyes glimmering, like christmas lights at night
tails curled, paws delicate, ears perked
the perfect pair of poise and passion
evil? nay, for feeling
the warmth of their bodies warms your heart like the smell of fresh cookies,
the lull of nighttime rain outside your window,
the bellyache of laughing with your best friend
evil? nay, they just
organize themselves neatly, settling their forms in careful order
like your mother putting away silverware after dinner
silver, gleaming teeth and claws
power to kill, but constrained to mincing your sister's baby blanket
evil? nay, isn't it plain? they are just as human as you or i
but, hiding a little more cunning behind their eyes
yes, i think cats will rule the world someday
and i accept my fate

My Question
by Amairani Ramirez

Running through my mind
Is it truly over?
I can't help but ask you this question ...
I don't mean to sound sad, I know I should keep my composure.
I wanted to take it all back when I saw your facial expression.
I can't help but ask you this question!
Please answer!
Just know I wanted to take it all back when I saw your facial expression.
I know I made this disaster
Please, please answer!
Is it necessary to turn off your phone?
I know I made this disaster ...
"Please leave a message at the tone."
Is it really that necessary to turn off your phone?
At least let me have my closure!
"Please leave a message at the tone."
"Hey ... it's me ... is it truly over?"

Scar Tissue
by Angelina Baxter

Green rubies that turn glancers to stone
piercing the soul, captivating the thoughts of temptation
the feelings are increased at the value of a smile
trapped in the sound of your voice
I don't wanna escape.
Palms touching, tracing the scars of not only your skin but your heart
needle and thread to completion
ripping & sewing
again & again
with my signature.
The breeze of malice air blowing into the field of dreams & desire
my ears are addicted to the sweet lies you say
tell me more
whisper to me our happily ever after
I'm slowly eating away the remains of our love.
I've heard that love makes people blind to the truth
I'll live in a lie if that lie is you.

Life's Questions
by Tianna Allen

Do not be afraid to ask questions
You must be curious now and then
Ever so philosophical, it's in our nature
Wonder if I'll go to college or be successful
How I'll function or what decisions I'll make
It'll be a long journey until I find out
Turn pages in books to gain knowledge usually helps
Out of the box is how I like to think
For those who are the most creative tend to inspire
You to do just that
In many ways
The words and ideas in my head usually
End up on paper, sooner or later
You may want to know what this was all about, and you may find out
If you read between the lines
Or will you?

Decision To Make
by Erica Furbush

Lost in my head; thoughts taking over.
Not knowing where to go
Never thought this far ahead
I need to find my next move
Not knowing where to go
People give me too many choices
I need to find my next move
Where would be the best place?
People give me too many choices
All different roads to take
Where would be the best place?
The future is a scary thought
All different roads to take
Not knowing where to go
The future is a scary thought
Lost in my head; thoughts taking over.

Tangles ...
by B'Elanna Powell

My yarn keeps getting all messed up
it keeps me from knitting freely
this will never look like a pup
I can't do this neatly
No! I can do this!
I must keep trying at least
I will have the bliss
of taming this beast!
But look at this mess,
is this a skein?
Is this a being of a dress?
It's being so mean!
Oh well, I'll have to just cut it and start again
for this is the pain of the craft
if you don't work hard you have nothing to gain
nothing else the lump of yarn will stop the cold draft

Nighttime Storms
by Cassidy Walters

I've always been afraid of storms in the night.
In the day they give me no fright.
It's when I'm alone and expected to sleep
That the thunder and lightning make me weep.
It's not that I'm scared of the storm itself
Or the sky as it's brown and gray with filth.
It's the danger that comes with the storm
Unlikely deaths that cause you to mourn.
One strike that gives a broken glass window,
Another that turns one's skin into baked dough.
The papers and such flying, gusts of wind,
The lightning cannot be dimmed.
I know this is all unlikely to happen.
But it's not very hard to imagine
Because when my mind starts to play
It won't stop until the sunshiny day.

Divorce - A Dead Tree
by Jordyn Johnson

My family is a tree late into fall
once blooming with color
but now dead and bare
My mother is the roots
bringing life to all of us
My siblings are the branches
entangling us all together
My dad is the dead leaves on the ground
no longer hanging on
I am the bark
brittle with despair

Invisible
by Hannah Laughery

I know you but you have never known me
I have walked alone on a path of darkness waiting for a light that I Never got
I've gone to places where nobody should ever have to go
Have been beaten and broken in ways nobody ever should have to be
In Vain I've tried to run from this fate
But fate just keeps dragging me back again and again
You ask me if I'm okay but I'm not and never will be
When the only reason I know I'm alive are my tiny insignificant footsteps
It will never be okay or fine or anything
I know what it's like to go through life feeling dead
Like you're not in your body but just drifting along
I'm not depressed, I'm just Stuck in a life I never wanted
Forced to do things I don't want to do
Somehow each day I have to wake up and keep going
Force myself to keep breathing throughout all the pain I've been dealt out
It's not death, but Believe me
It's an even worse state of being
You end up Losing yourself to the everlasting cages of deceit
Till who you are is just a memory of someone who used to be
I know you but you will never Ever know me

Never Forget
by Kaitlyn Angel

Never forget that I love you
Even if we are
Very far apart
Even if we never see each other
Remember the good times we had and

Forget all the bad
Often I'm writing you letters to
Remind you that I love you
Get ready for the future because
Eventually you're coming home
That way our family will be complete

The Beautiful and Messed Up Place Where I Belong
by Autumn Bakker

I am from windmills, from dancing in festivals,
And from tulips and stargazer lilies.
I am from horror movies and gore.
I'm from deep waters and heavy waves,
That thrashed against my legs on sandy beaches.
I'm from thingamajigs and whosie whatsits,
The she started it and I'm finishing its.
From the blueberry fields and the apple orchards,
I'm from lighthouses, and the pentagram below the stairs.
I'm from *Station 11, American Pie, & Red Dawn.*
From messy bed sheets and clothes on the floor.
From the leg my grandfather limps on,
And that spot where I ran over my grandmother.
I'm from the tired days and dreamless nights.
From pirouettes, pliés and arabesques,
And the 99 cent drugstore pop from across the street.
I am from those moments,
Where two people probably shouldn't have ended up together, but did,
And are happy with the kids they've made, and each other.
I am from a broken seed, that's been fortified to be stronger than before,
And isn't gonna break again.

Stress Breaks
by Jasmine Stallard

Going through life you have to deal with a lot of stress.
Sometimes, I feel like the world is always against me.
I try to keep all my feelings in but, the more and more I do,
the more and more I crack.
I am in pieces.
I am just shards, scattered all over the floor,
with water drops oozing out of them.
Then, I find some way to write down the things that caused my shattering.
I am whole again.
I am no longer in pieces.
Then, the process repeats.

Timeless
by Avery Escajeda

Time is not eternal
Short and quick, always on the move
Held together by strings of choice
Free will could destroy it all
Short and quick, always on the move
People travel with no destination
Free will could destroy it all
A young heart is much too fragile
People travel with no destination
Screaming and shouting when things don't go their way
A young heart is much too fragile
Time is not eternal

I Hear Roots Creaking
by Isaac Kroll

I hear roots creaking, those of our days of old,
Tying us to inescapable fates, based on neither deed nor word.
The willow sways with childhood plays, memories of the beginning,
Yet though its branches are intact, the roots are ever-leaking.
Water dripping from a spout, ripples in the rain,
The impact is, to most, unseen, but still, it doth remain.
Retaining heritage of the pool from which it once did flow,
The splitting of words down to their roots cannot contain the whole.
For though these words of fragment parts may be defined by their means,
The origins hold inequity to a product now set free.
To this end I will valiantly contend, despite forces to confine,
As fog gives way to nurtured plants, so will be my clear skies.

Golden Hearts
by Katherine Newman

Begone with the sands! Begone with the snake in a bush!
The sun beats down upon stones,
Stones stacked upon stones,
Built by hands beaten by time.
Beats upon sands shifting with time and blood
There's a bush on the horizon, it's hiding the sun,
The sun that relentlessly sweats down upon the stones
Built by bloody beaten hands.
Feet tread sands marred by snakes in a bush! They go with the sands!
There's stones with blood in them; yet they won't give up secrets!
They're sweating and bleeding and weeping-
They're following shifting sands and dying stars across oceans that don't weep
They don't and won't; can't; weep for them so they follow a bird marred against
Horizon that bleeds stone and sun and sweat!
Birds made of golden feathers and a thousand eyes whisper out secrets
They lull in the most vulnerable snakes and snap them in half;
leave them hissing out
Words only the snakes could ever know how to make, like how to make
Stones weep blood and sweat!

The Great American Dream
by Peter Moon

Freedom to speak, freedom to read,
Freedom to think, freedom to lead.
The freedom of life and liberty.
Given to us by an omniscient deity.
Opposed by the few, loved by the many,
Rescuers from oppression and tyranny.
Established to harbor pilgrims and refugees,
Accepts and houses those from instability.
And carries the weight of every municipality.
God bless this land, God bless its people.
Give them protection, against all evil.
Make them powerful, to provide aid.
Allow them comfort, to express grace.
Give them a history, long and great.
From Hawaii to Florida, from Alaska to Guam,
Let it all prosper, that it may live long.
So that none will wander, and all will visit.
Let their freedom ring, and let their children sing,
Of the great America, of this great dream.

Bottle Return
by Megan Clark

I've been kicked around
Many dents accumulated on my frame
You decide to return me, it won't work.
Oh my figure is not redeemable
They will not accept me
What I am— it spits me out,
Don't try again, it will only further destroy my self image.
Find a can that has no dents
Try her out,
Perfection can't be rejected
I don't fit your mold,
Perfect is outside of my reach
But she's in yours.
Her worth is superficial.
Her interest is a façade.
Her image may be what you want, but I'll always be what you crave

My Type
by Caleb A. Dixon

My people are my type
The type that run around open fire hydrants, but be back by the streetlights
The type that rap about going from the trenches to the spotlight
The type that fix cars by hearing what it sound like
My people are artists
work the hardest
Talk the loudest
But have the most prowess
My people make it do what it do
Yea we might rep red or we might rep blue
And staying in homes is something we may or may not do
But through thick and through thin we ride for our crew
My people ride low riders to show they the mack
My people shoot dice, and ball on the blacktop and talk smack
My people got down and out, but will be back
Never forget that you can always bet on black

With Only Me
by Olivia Holloway

Listen to me, for what I have to say.
Talk with me, so we can share interests.
Laugh with me, let's have some fun.
Fight with me, so we'll voice our opinions.
Compromise with me, we'll make an agreement.
Stay with me, you'll be my partner in crime.
Commit to me, so you'll be all mine.
Treat me, for I like being spoiled sometimes.
Cry with me, we'll comfort one another.
Hold me, so we can feel each other's warmth.
Love me, I'll give you my everything.
Kiss me, we'll surrender to one another.
Caress me, give me all your passion.
Run with me, we'll chase our future.

The Kiss of the Cosmos
by Chantel Bretzinger

I can feel it in my bones when I dance
under the pale moonlight, wrapping
myself in the familiar.
I can feel it in my blood when comets streak
the sky, ladders I could use to escape.
I can feel it on my flesh as the sun blisters
the Earth, yet I remain unmarked.
I can feel it in my heart when the stars die,
the hollowing of someone who could never be whole here.
I can feel it in my mind when I stare at the night sky,
knowing I was never meant for this world.
I was born to weave my soul through the mysteries
of the cosmos and allow myself to be consumed
by starlight.

A Letter To Anxiety
by Elizabeth Williams

dear you,

you are clouds,
seemingly innocent at first with your white, light airiness.
on my perfect days you float across clear skies,
sneaking into the blue that i so cherish
and before i know it, you are everywhere.
but then you develop, change, into something more sinister.
so quickly you turn dark
and every direction i look, you await me.
you grow and expand across my once beautiful sky
infecting that blue with the darkest grays
and there's no escaping your oncoming storm.
it's on those days that i recall the feeling
of having no heart in my chest
yet still having a pulse.
why can't you leave me be?

with no amount of love,
    elizabeth

Where I Am From
by Aidana Dogdurbaeva

I am from the World,
I am from the continent called Asia,
This place for me is Wonderland,
I am from the heart of Asia.
From the country of mountains,
Country of the beautiful nature,
The beauty of nature is countless,
Country with a great culture.
I am from the land of hospitality,
I was born in the land of animals,
My land is rich with animality.
Born happy to be called Kyrgyz,
To have such traditions,
To be so brave and fearless,
To have these weather conditions.
I am from the land of great food,
Land, where food is organic,
Recipes which come from the broods,
Food which you eat and get manic.
I am from the land of my future,
I am from Kyrgyzstan!

Different
by Isabella Granados

Different is good
Different is okay
Different is acceptable
Some choose to be different
Others don't
Yet in the end
You're still human
You're still someone
You still have a voice
And you can still dream and become something you want to be
You can still love and be loved
You can be you
You do not need to hide anymore
You do not need to feel ashamed or judged
If you block out all the negative around you
You see yourself become someone you never thought you could be
Being different is amazing
Because you are your own person
You are unique in every way
You are different and that's okay

The Good Life
by Talia Tetmeyer

Every morning she sits at her beautiful desk.
Every morning she applies layers upon layers of makeup.
Every morning she listens as videos tell her how perfect she is.
Every morning she puts a purple ribbon in her hair.
Every day she goes to school.
Every day her friends tell her how she has the "funny" dad.
Every day she laughs it off.
But every night she has to come home.
Every night she takes off the makeup.
Every night she cowers in the corner.
Every night the "funny" dad tells her all of her flaws.
Every night the "funny" dad beats her.
You see,
The makeup was only to cover her scars
The beautiful room was only a façade
The videos were so she didn't believe him
The "friends" were oblivious to the horrendous abuse.
The "good life" wasn't so good after all.

Eraser
by Jaden Copeland

You were always my best friend
You would fix every error
Make it seem as if it never happened
The day comes though
Where I wrote too hard
I went to my eraser
But it was not enough
After the vigorous erasing
There was still that faint image of the words
Eventually you were gone
Shredded to pieces
And there I was
Left guilty and shameful
For the one thing I trusted was now gone

Breathe
by Briana Jones

Head spinning, eyes blurring,
Mouth dry, ears ringing,
I can't breathe.
Legs numb, arms sore,
Back tense, neck stiff,
I can't breathe.
Falling, slipping,
Crawling, stopping,
I can't breathe.
Eyes dark, sounds gone,
Taste nothing, feel empty,
I can't breathe.
Tears fall, sweat pours,
Blood drips, drowned by fear,
I can't breathe.
Eyes go blank, body grows cold,
Skin so pale, heart beats its last,
I'm not breathing.

Polluted
by Kendra Rankin

A small little cloud is up in the sky,
growing bigger and bigger as time goes by.
This cloud isn't normal, this cloud isn't right.
Filled with toxins and smoke, it makes quite a sight.
This cloud was created and turned to a beast,
Eating the sky and having a feast.
Above all our heads there is only smoke,
We take a breath and then we choke.
The cloud is all around us, it turned to a fog.
It stole all our air, its being a hog.
Blinded and gagging, we look for fresh air,
We all cannot stand it, it's more than we can bear.
We put out the fires, and turn off our cars,
The fog is getting thinner we can see the stars.
We turn off the engine, and shutdown the plants
This small little cloud is done with its rant.

Holding Crushed Diamonds
by Phil Meup

I have so much to gain yet so much to lose.
Imperfect emotions reflect hopeful hues.
I take every pleasure in my understanding.
Please hold on tight, my plane is crash landing.
If all that is earned is eventually taken,
Then death steals all life; I'm continually shaken.
Salvation gets Heaven, rejection gets Hell.
I want life eternal, my lover as well.
I have so much to gain yet so much to lose.
I need God, I have God, I know God, I love God.
Necessity, Longing and loyalty clash.
I want you, I have you, forever I'll love you.
At end of time it's God over all.
As sands still flow I'll follow His call.
But Death takes the beauty I've found in its fall.

3rd Place

Emma Tafazoli

Atelophobia: Motaassefam, Baba
(Forgive Me, Father)
by Emma Tafazoli

I shot my world across the floor from a crystal cannon,
and tried to clean the mess I made with a broken brush.
You've come to hate my disarray; I know that you can't stand it.
I see the ire of cold contempt behind the green of lush.
The battle cry of haunting time hidden by a hush.
Clean it, clean it, clean it, so it doesn't show too much.
Spotless floors, charging Moors, the dust will find its casket.
Blood and tears from distant peers trade years in woven baskets.
He loomed and lumbered, the Persian King, who never had enough,
Down the track, he tore my heart and called it reckless love,
so with distaste pushed back inside she steps into the mess,
collects my body once again to lay it down to rest.

2nd Place

Christina Tillinghast

The Big Bang
by Christina Tillinghast

the words slid from her grasp and broke into a million blazing pieces,
glittering crystal shards exploding heavens
onto the ethereal kitchen tile, drawing blood
she had forgotten that the words were dangling dangerously
from painted fingertips,
forgotten how deeply they desired destruction,
to kiss the ground and remain eternally embedded
in the discolored grout and dusty corners
part of her wished she could take them back, wished she could say
"I'm sorry" or "I didn't mean it"
but she wasn't and she did
she knew the Big Bang was irreversible, that the unleashed light
and celestial dust could no longer return to its high-density state
there was no going back to the pent-up objections
and unspoken bitterness –
no – space was to constantly expand, spreading the matter and heat
through the breadth of time and across the kitchen floor
until they engulfed whatever was before
and became all that had ever existed
until they consumed her parents' fallen faces
and filled her own shaking lungs
and as she stared in awe of the wreckage,
her nascent universe taking shape,
regret and relief playfully competed to sweep away at the fragments

1st Place

Irura Nyiha

Irura Nyiha is a 16-year-old senior, originally from Nairobi, Kenya
who enjoys math, robotics, physics and astrophysics.
She is the co-head of her school's Quizbowl
and is a member of the local chapter of the African Student Union.
More than anything, Irura loves to read and write.
She says writing poetry allows her to express
her thoughts and feelings and is a comfort of sorts.
She credits her favorite poet,
W.B. Yeats as her inspiration to never stop writing.
Congratulations, Irura!

She Speaks In Cursive
by Irura Nyiha

She speaks in cursive
Every single letter from those pursed lips
A chrysalis of splendor
Little droplets, soft and tender
Speaks in cursive,
In melody, calligraphy
A voice that floats upon the winds
A perfect, formless entity
In cursive,
She paints a picture-perfect scene
A blossoming of harmony
Cadenza in soliloquy
Cursive,
A chorus of chirality
Her cry, a fading beauty
And her laughter, sweetened poetry.

Index
of
Authors

● ● ● ● ● ● ● ● ● ● ● ● ● ● ●

Index of Authors

Index of Authors

Index of Authors

Index of Authors

Illustrious
Price List

Initial Copy 32.95

Additional Copies 25.00

Please Enclose $7 Shipping/Handling Each Order

Must specify book title and name of student author

Check or Money Order Payable to:

The America Library of Poetry
P.O. Box 978
Houlton, Maine 04730

Please Allow 4-8 Weeks For Delivery

THE AMERICA
LIBRARY OF POETRY

www.libraryofpoetry.com

Email: generalinquiries@libraryofpoetry.com